Typical and Atypical Child and Adolescent Development 5

Communication and Language Development

This concise guide offers an accessible introduction to the development of communication and language in infancy and childhood. It integrates insights from both typical and atypical development to reveal the fundamental aspects of human growth and development, and common developmental disorders.

The topic books in this series draw on international research in the field and are informed by biological, social and cultural perspectives, offering explanations of developmental phenomena with a focus on how children and adolescents at different ages actually think, feel and act. In this volume, Stephen von Tetzchner explains key topics including: Language and Communication; early development of communication; theories of communicative development; early dialogues; gestures; the development of language; language in use; child-directed language; gender differences multilingualism and language in other modalities; and language disorders.

Together with a companion website that offers topic-based quizzes, lecturer PowerPoint slides and sample essay questions, *Typical and Atypical Child and Adolescent Development 5 Communication and Language Development* is an essential text for all students of developmental psychology, as well as those working in the fields of child development, developmental disabilities and special education.

Stephen von Tetzchner is Professor of Developmental Psychology at the Department of Psychology, University of Oslo, Norway.

T0347490

The content of this topic book is taken from Stephen von Tetzchner's core textbook *Child and Adolescent Psychology: Typical and Atypical Development*. The comprehensive volume offers a complete overview of child and adolescent development – for more information visit www.routledge.com/9781138823396

Topics from Child and Adolescent Psychology Series
Stephen von Tetzchner

The **Topics from Child and Adolescent Psychology Series** offers concise guides on key aspects of child and adolescent development. They are formed from selected chapters from Stephen von Tetzchner's comprehensive textbook *Child and Adolescent Psychology: Typical and Atypical Development* and are intended to be accessible introductions for students of relevant modules on developmental psychology courses, as well as for professionals working in the fields of child development, developmental disabilities and special education. The topic books explain the key aspects of human development by integrating insights from typical and atypical development to cement understanding of the processes involved and the work with children who have developmental disorders. They examine sensory, physical and cognitive disabilities and the main emotional and behavioural disorders of childhood and adolescence, as well as the developmental consequences of these disabilities and disorders.

Topics books in the series

Typical and Atypical Child and Adolescent Development 1
Theoretical Perspectives and Methodology

Typical and Atypical Child and Adolescent Development 2
Genes, Fetal Development and Early Neurological Development

Typical and Atypical Child and Adolescent Development 3
Perceptual and Motor Development

Typical and Atypical Child and Adolescent Development 4
Cognition, Intelligence and Learning

Typical and Atypical Child and Adolescent Development 5
Communication and Language Development

Typical and Atypical Child and Adolescent Development 6
Emotions, Temperament, Personality, Moral, Prosocial and Antisocial Development

Typical and Atypical Child and Adolescent Development 7
Social Relations, Self-awareness and Identity

For more information on individual topic books visit https://www.routledge.com/Topics-from-Child-and-Adolescent-Psychology/book-series/TFCAAP

Typical and Atypical Child and Adolescent Development 5

Communication and Language Development

Stephen von Tetzchner

Routledge
Taylor & Francis Group
LONDON AND NEW YORK

Cover image: Westend61/Westend61 via Getty Images.

First published 2023
by Routledge
4 Park Square, Milton Park, Abingdon, Oxon OX14 4RN

and by Routledge
605 Third Avenue, New York, NY 10158

*Routledge is an imprint of the Taylor & Francis Group, an
informa business*

© 2023 Stephen von Tetzchner

British Library Cataloguing-in-Publication Data
A catalogue record for this book is available from the British Library

Library of Congress Cataloging-in-Publication Data
A catalog record has been requested for this book

ISBN: 978-1-032-27397-6 (hbk)
ISBN: 978-1-032-26777-7 (pbk)
ISBN: 978-1-003-29252-4 (ebk)

DOI: 10.4324/9781003292524

Typeset in Bembo
by Apex CoVantage, LLC

Access the companion website: www.routledge.com/cw/vonTetzchner

Contents

Introduction

Communication and language are essential human abilities, and the use of language distinguishes humans from other species. Communication may be non-verbal but language is inconceivable without communication. Language allows humans to share what they think about, stories, desires, ideas, feelings and so on. Humans use language in most activities and language is both part of the culture and a tool for acquiring social and cultural knowledge. Children acquire communication and language skills within a social and relational framework that changes as they grow older.

Development can be defined as an age-related process involving changes in the structure and functions of humans and other species. The 12 parts of this topic book present core issues related to the development of communication and language, building on the models of development and the developmental way of thinking presented in Book 1, *Theoretical Perspectives and Methodology*. Most individual differences in mental and physical features and abilities do not emerge directly from a particular biological or environmental factor but rather as a result of *interaction effects*, where biological and environmental factors are moderated by one or several other factors. Moreover, development is never a one-way process: it is a *transactional process*, characterized by reciprocal influences between the child and the environment over time. Readers may find it useful to consult the part on developmental models in Book 1, *Theoretical Perspectives and Methodology*, or the corresponding chapters in the complete book before reading the present topic book.

The present topic book includes both typical communication and language development, which is the most common course with unimpaired functions and ordinary individual differences between children, and atypical development, which represents various degrees of unusual or irregular development, including the development of children and adolescents who have communication and language disorders. The issues presented in this topic book are particularly relevant for teachers, special educators and other staff in preschool and school. Their task is to support children's play and learning, and insight into the development of communication and language is necessary for adapting educational strategies to each pupil's needs.

Human development to maturity stretches over about 20 years. Basic communication and language skills emerge during the first years of life but language continues to develop through childhood and adolescence. The basic apparatus for communication and language is shared by nearly all humans but there are considerable individual differences in communication and language abilities. Some children are early talkers, while others are slower but reach the same level of language competence. Some children have communication and language disorders with delayed development and some may never reach the linguistic level of their peers.

Communication originates in infants' ability to focus attention and a sensory system where stimulation from other people has attentional value over other forms of stimulation (see Book 3, *Perceptual and Motor Development, Part 1*). The infants' social attention evolves gradually into joint attention with others. Infants and toddlers may follow the gaze direction of adults to find out what they are attentive to, or look back and forth between an object and the adult to be sure they have the same attentional focus as themselves. The theories of communication development focus on the process from attention orienting to attention regulated by social interaction, and the establishment of joint social attention and engagement. Pointing directs attention to particular locations or things and is usually children's first communicative gesture, soon to be followed by symbolic gestures and the first words.

Theories of language development must be able to describe and explain typical language development and the variation that can be observed in children's language development. The main theories presented in this topic book differ in their descriptions of linguistic processes, in the role they attribute to genes and experience, in their assumptions about what sets humans apart from species that do not have language, and in how the acquisition process proceeds. Much of the discussion is about grammatical competence. There is a main distinction between nativism and the other theories presented here.

According to nativism, language development only requires that children are exposed to a language. The other theoretical directions assume that grammatical competence to a greater extent is a result of children's active use of language, but have different explanations of how children acquire language and to some extent focus on different aspects of language development. There is also a main distinction between behaviorism and the other theories: behaviorism sees language as learned behavior while the other theories emphasize the cognitive processes involved in language comprehension and use. The considerable disagreements about the bases of even basic language skills reflect the complexity of human communication and language.

Speech sounds are part of children's auditory environment even before birth, and children's perception of speech changes significantly through the first couple of years. As part of the cultural adaptation, infants lose their early ability to distinguish between most speech sounds while becoming better able to distinguish between sounds that differentiate word meanings in their language or languages – a large part of the World's children grow up with two or more languages. Speech production follows a path where children's speech gradually becomes more similar to the language or languages that are spoken in the environment. The children learn to divide the voice stream into meaning-bearing elements and understand which people, objects, events and so on are relevant to what is being said. Children who learn sign language must be able to identify signs in the flow of hand movements they see and attach meaning to them.

Joint attention and speech or sign perception constitute a basis for inferring the meaning of words or signs. The acquisition of the first words is a quite slow process in most children but the speed soon increases and remains high throughout childhood and adolescence. Children learn the common words of their society but the content of their vocabularies varies both at an early age and later, reflecting differences in the children's interests, activities, education and cultural background. Also gender and social economic background may influence children's language development. Moreover, it is not only the number of words that increases, the comprehension and use of the words change dynamically over time, including metaphorical and other forms of figurative use. Adults also learn new words but the addition of new vocabulary items slows down with age.

The ability to combine words to relay new messages is the hallmark of human language. Combining words allows children to produce both more specific and more complex messages. The transition from single-word utterances to multi-word utterances is therefore an essential milestone on children's way to comprehension and production of language. Grammars differ between languages and children learn to use word order, inflections and grammatical words to express gradually more complex meanings, using a variety of strategies. The theories differ in how they interpret both errors and lack of errors as the child's competence increases.

Children learn the language(s) around them. They learn from observing others and through the answers other people give to their utterances. However, learning from others' language use does not mean that language development is a simple process of imitation. Internalization of the language conventions is only part of language competence; equally important is externalization, expressing personal knowledge and ideas which without language would not have been possible to transmit to others.

The acquisition of words and grammatical knowledge is based on an understanding of the functions of language, that is, how language may be used for various communicative purposes. The conversation may be regarded as the basic unit of language use. Words and sentences are rarely used in isolation but rather as part of shorter or longer conversations already from the early adult-child dialogues. Conversational skills include initiating and ending the conversation, taking turns, changing topics, correcting mistakes and negotiating meaning. These skills emerge as a blend of children's earlier communication and language skills, concept formation, and social skills. Early conversations typically concern things children and adults are doing or have done together, such as farm animals in a picture book, the food the adult is cooking, the peers at nursery school, and so on. Over time, the children's contributions become more autonomous and less dependent on the adults' help and chaining together.

In all societies, humans communicate about people and events, including gossip. Children start early to share experiences, comment on ongoing events and talk about past and future events with guidance from the parents. Narratives are a natural extension of these conversations, often co-constructed with parents or other adults. Construction of narratives constitutes an important part of children's language development and is a basis for learning about the world and the development of autobiographical memory. Adults adapt their language in child-directed language to facilitate the child's understanding and learning of words, grammar and conversational skills. With age, children's narratives become more independent and coherent, and the content changes as children move into adolescence.

Speech is the most common language mode but language may take different forms. The national sign languages have developed mainly through the linguistic praxis of individuals with severe hearing impairment and their families. Individuals with normal hearing who are severely delayed in speech development or who fail to develop intelligible speech can learn to express themselves with manual signs or graphic symbols.

Language is complex, and various factors may slow down or hinder language development. Some children struggle with acquiring spoken or signed language (see Book 1, *Theoretical Perspectives and Methodology, Part IV*). The importance of communication and language for everyday functioning and participation in social and societal life implies that disorders of communication and language may have a severe impact on all aspects of life, education, work, relations, and the well-being of children and adolescents. Many children need help and support in the early phases of language development and some may need language intervention also into adolescence. Children with language disorders may also struggle with reading and writing (see Book 4, *Cognition, Intelligence and Learning, Part VI*).

Some of the terminology used in developmental psychology may be unfamiliar to some readers. Many of these terms can be found in the Glossary.

1

Language and Communication

Language consists of a unique system of **symbols** and grammar that only humans use to communicate, and that distinguishes human beings from other species. The length of this topic book reflects both the complexity of the language development process and the fact that language is a core element in human social life. The **development** of **communication** precedes that of language and represents the core function of language. For children to be able to learn to comprehend and use spoken language, they must be able to divide the flow of speech into meaningful units and understand the relevance of objects, people, and events in the environment to the speech sounds they hear. Children who learn sign language must be able to divide the stream of hand movements they observe and attribute meaning to them. They must understand their use and the intentions behind them when other people – and eventually they themselves – use language.

DOI: 10.4324/9781003292524-1

2

Early Development of Communication

In **communication** development the human ability to regulate attention is integrated with *social orientation*. Visual and auditory preferences lead children to direct their attention at stimulation from other people (see Book 3, *Perceptual and Motor Development*, Part I), while children's early emotional **signals**, such as smiling and crying, attract the attention of adults (see Book 6, *Emotions, Temperament, Personality, Moral, Prosocial and Antisocial Development*, Chapter 6 p. 6). Communication emerges as children become able to engage in **joint attention**, seek to direct the attention of others, and let their own attention be directed by others, that is, when the child's action is based on a **communicative intention**, or when the child perceives that others have such an intention (Rommetveit, 1974). It is a transactional process where child and parent influence each other.

Joint Attention

Infants are aware of other people's faces and eyes at an early age, and even newborns look longer at faces that are turned toward them than at faces that look away (Csibra, 2010). At the same time, the direction in which the child gazes provides parents with an important *clue* to the child's focus of attention. They often pick up toys their child is looking at (Collis and Schaffer, 1975), and 50–70 percent of the time they introduce the name of the child's object of interest (Woodward and Markman, 1998).

The first sign that children begin to become aware of others' attention is that they begin to follow their facial orientation and gaze direction. There seems to be a development from attention to the adult to

DOI: 10.4324/9781003292524-2

attention to the environment and to what the attention of the adult informs them about the environment. Observations of interactions between 6-week-olds and their mothers showed that they were oriented toward one another 70 percent of the time. At 6 months of age, this had decreased to 30 percent, and a greater proportion of interaction involved objects within reaching distance (Kaye and Fogel, 1980). These changes are also reflected in parental speech, which at this age begins to revolve less around the child's state and more on the child's actions, as well as on objects and events in the environment (Snow, 1977).

There is a gradual change in the alignment and function of attention. While interacting, parents and children often look at the same object, but during the first few months it is the parents who follow the child's focus of attention. At 6 months, children begin to move their gaze toward the same side of the room the adult is looking at, but stop at the first thing that catches their interest. At 9 months, children are able to locate the object an adult is looking at as long as it lies within their field of vision. At this age, children also begin to check whether the adult is looking at them or at what they themselves are looking at. At 12 months, a child's ability to follow an adult's gaze direction is relatively well established, but still depends on where the object is located in relation to the child. Around 18 months, children are mostly – but not always – able to follow another person's gaze, independent of the direction in which the other person is looking (MacPherson and Moore, 2007; Mundy et al., 2007). There are, however, significant **individual differences** in when children begin to follow the gaze direction of others.

Other people are children's main source of knowledge about the world; children need strategies to monitor and capture the attention of others in order to understand and react to the events around them (Nelson, 2007b). In joint attention the child and the adult are both attentive to the same thing, for example a toy, *and* aware of each other's attention (Carpenter and Liebal, 2011). Adults often use the child's visual attention and interest as clues to ensure that the child perceives the relevant communicative expressions, and they lead the child's awareness to those aspects of the situation that are relevant to what the adult is saying. Activities involving verbal communication provide children with cues to what the adult is saying and how their own expressions are understood.

Most descriptions of early communicative development focus on joint visual attention because visual situational cues are most prominent for children at this age (Begeer et al., 2014). Nonetheless, the use of vision is not an essential condition for joint attention. Blind children, too, establish joint attention to objects and events with other people, but for the children to understand what the parents are communicating about, they must be given non-visual cues (Bigelow, 2003; Pérez-Pereira and Conti-Ramsden, 1999). The parents must use the child's listening behavior and manual exploration as clues to the child's focus of attention – blind children use the fingers to explore (Fraiberg, 1977). Thus, joint attention is equally important to blind and sighted children, but differs in the use of experiential modalities. This also demonstrates that communication is extremely robust. Even if children are unable to see, they will attribute communicative intent to the sounds of their parents' voices.

In early **infancy**, children are used to having the attention of the people around them when they are awake. As children begin to move independently, they find that this is less and less the case. Once they begin to take direct action to establish joint attention – they may even turn their mother's head in their own direction while she talks to someone else – it not only reflects their awareness of other people's attention, but also the discovery that others may have a different focus of attention than their own.

Joint Attention and Autism

Children with **autism spectrum disorder** are characterized by problems related to communication and social interaction (see Book 1, *Theoretical Perspectives and Methodology*, Chapter 32). Inadequately developed non-verbal communication and joint attention skills are important early indications when screening for or diagnosing autism (Kim and Lord, 2013; Stenberg et al., 2014). However, the problems are not absolute. With increasing age, most children with autism engage in situations involving joint attention but are less likely than other children to lead the attention of other people to something just to show them what has captured their interest. Their early communication is usually more **instrumental** than **declarative** (Camaioni et al., 2003; Naber et al., 2008). Why children with autism develop these types of problems is still unknown, but there is reason to believe that their difficulties acquiring language are related to their problems with communication (Sarria et al., 1996). When children have difficulties following the cues to other people's attention, they will generally also struggle with the formation of meaning itself. Therefore, many early intervention programs for children with autism spectrum disorder aim to engage them in situations involving joint attention (Chang et al., 2016; Jones et al., 2006; Murza et al., 2016).

3

Theories of Communicative Development

Most theorists believe that communication has an innate basis, that there is something about human biology that makes communication possible, but precisely what is assumed to be innate varies considerably. According to Bloom (1998), human beings have an innate motive to create and maintain **intersubjectivity** – a drive to share knowledge about facts, ideas, emotions and so on, and thereby establish their **self** in a social world. Trevarthen (1979, 2015) explains joint attention by proposing that intersubjectivity is innate and that children are intrinsically motivated to share emotions and experiences. The ability to communicate evolves in a way comparable to the heart and other internal organs. According to Trevarthen, infants as young as 2–3 months of age are capable of **primary intersubjectivity**, in which attention is directed at the person they are engaged with and they can understand communicative expressions as well as the effect of their own expressions on others, for example that they can tease someone. However, Trevarthen's theory of primary intersubjectivity remains controversial since it implies that 2-month-olds are able to perceive their effect on others as well as the fact that others are aware of them. Most theorists believe that this type of communicative understanding and insight into the minds of other people develops much later. **Secondary intersubjectivity** appears around the age of 9 months, according to Trevarthen. It manifests itself when children and adults are attentive to something outside themselves, for example, an object or animal, and each is aware of the other's attention. There is general agreement about this form of intersubjectivity.

Tomasello (1999, 2003) argues that human beings have a species-specific ability to "read" the *intentions* of others, an ability present

DOI: 10.4324/9781003292524-3

from the moment the child exhibits the first communicative expressions at the end of the first year. He points to the fact that the child's perception of a movement or a sound as a communicative act always requires the attribution of communicative intent. Otherwise, the sounds coming from another person's mouth, or their gestural movements, would remain meaningless. According to Tomasello (2008), this type of understanding does not have its origins in an innate social motive, such as Trevarthen and Bloom argue, but in the human propensity for cooperation and children's general cognitive and social skills.

4

Early Dialogues

A *dialogue* is a communicative interaction – verbal or non-verbal – between two people who share the same focus of attention and somehow convey something and adapt to each other. The earliest dialogues largely take place in the context of play and daily routines in which the child and adult take turns and the adult facilitates and helps the child solve communicative "problems" (see Scollon, 1976, 2001). Often it is the adult who initiates play and routines that involve turntaking, but it is precisely the adult's ability to adapt that allows the child to take the lead and contribute to early dialogue (Bruner, 1975). The routines themselves are not the goal of communication but provide a framework that allows children to acquire skills they later can apply outside of these routines. Early interactions require a certain degree of repetition and **stability**, based as they are on the child's knowledge of the world, and routine activities provide this stability (Nelson, 2007a). Many early intervention programs are based on routine activities (Hughes-Scholes and Gavidia-Payne, 2016).

Infants exhibit many actions and expressions before they show actions with a communicative intent. They do not yet communicate in the strict sense of the word – communication requires expressions to be intentional, and there is no evidence that children actually attempt to convey information or otherwise influence the attention of the adult. However, the actions help adults attribute interests and emotional reactions to the child, and see infants as social individuals and engage them in dialogues (Goldstein and West, 1999).

DOI: 10.4324/9781003292524-4

5

Gestures

Manual **gestures** are hand movements primarily used for communication, and interpreted consistently within a social system (Kendon, 2004; Morris et al., 1979). **Deictic** or **pointing gestures** direct attention in a certain direction or toward something in the environment without naming it, and can be translated as "there" or "that." **Symbolic gestures** function more like words and specify or name what the gesture refers to. Children may, for example, ask to be picked up by stretching their hands up to the adult. Later, the same wish may be expressed by saying *Up!* or *Sit lap!* The acquisition of gestures is an important milestone in the development of communication, since the goal of the child's actions goes beyond mere physical interaction with the environment. The function of gestures is to direct the attention – or the mind – of another human being (Tomasello et al., 2007).

Pointing

When the child starts to follow pointing gestures, this provides the first clue that a child understands someone else's communication. Pointing indicates a direction for the child's attention, and an understanding of pointing involves the ability to perceive the intent behind the pointing gesture. When adults point at something, infants initially look at the extended hand without moving their eyes in the direction of the point, suggesting that they do not understand the gestural properties of the pointing handshape. Some 9-month-olds are able to look in the right direction when this does not involve having to turn around, but most infants look at the hand. If a little older children have to shift their gaze further to the side or turn their head to see where the adult is pointing, they just as often look in another direction (Desrochers et al., 1995).

DOI: 10.4324/9781003292524-5

When infants look in the right direction, but do not follow the pointing gesture all the way to its target, it may indicate that their perception of the other person's intentions continues to be vague (Lock et al., 1990; Tomasello et al., 2007). Not until the age of about 14 months do the majority of children consistently follow the direction of the point, and somewhat later they usually look in the right direction no matter where the adult is pointing (Desrochers et al., 1995).

Pointing is usually also the child's first communicative gesture and the clearest form of **prelinguistic** communication about objects in the environment. Pointing with an extended index finger usually does not occur until the age of 9–10 months and becomes more common after the age of 12 months, with major individual differences. Some 8-month-olds exhibit this type of pointing gesture, but it is not unusual for children to start pointing as late as 16 months of age (Butterworth, 2003). Unlike reaching, the communicative function of pointing becomes evident in that children increasingly look at the adult when pointing (Figure 5.1). At around 12 months of age, children also vocalize more often in connection with pointing and gaze when an adult looks in a direction other than that of the object they are interested in themselves, making their attempts to communicate become more effective because the sound draws the adult's attention to the pointing gesture (Legerstee and Barillas, 2003).

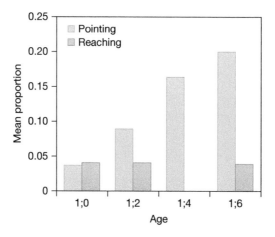

Figure 5.1 The communicative function of pointing.

Pointing is a core element of early dialogues.

Pointing and reaching undergo different functional developments. Pointing has a communicative function: to lead others to do or become attentive to something. The purpose of reaching is to obtain something for oneself. Between 12 and 18 months, children increasingly look at the adult when pointing, while the incidence of gazing at the adult when reaching for something does not increase (based on Franco and Butterworth, 1996, p. 320).

Pointing is *referential* and always involves a meaningful context. The purpose of **declarative** pointing is to inform or share an experience. Many 12-month-olds will point at the item an adult pretends to be looking for, and may also point when something disappears (Liszkowski et al., 2006; Tomasello, 2008). **Instrumental** or **imperative** pointing aims to induce the other person to carry out a specific action, such as giving something to the child or removing something. In addition, pointing may be *exploratory*. When pointing at an object the adult is already looking at, the child seems to request information: get an object label, find out how something works, if it safe or dangerous, and so on. Pointing thus becomes a tool for cultural learning that provides the child with new or corroborating information from knowledgeable adults (Southgate et al., 2007).

There are several explanations for how children learn to point. According to Vygotsky (1962), pointing gestures arise from what he calls the "**ritualization** of action": the child tries to reach for something but cannot get hold of it. An adult observes the reaching action and retrieves the object for the child. Consequently, the child discovers that the movement can be used to get others to fetch things that are out of reach. This, however, only explains the development of imperative pointing – pointing to get something. Another explanation is that children learn to point by imitating others, but observations of children's interactions with adults who point do not indicate that imitation plays a major role. Besides, children often use pointing movements *before* showing an understanding of others' pointing gestures (Carpendale and Carpendale, 2010; Tomasello, 2008).

Shinn (1900) views pointing as an extension of children's earliest experiences with touch and exploration with their fingertips. This is in line with studies that have found a significant increase in the **incidence** of pointing gestures around 18 months, an age that sees a corresponding increase in explorative behavior (Goldin-Meadow, 2015). Carpendale and Carpendale (2010) integrate the theories of Vygotsky and Shinn, based on the assumption that the precursors to pointing can both be found in children's attempts to reach for things and their exploration of things with the fingertips. By interacting with adults, children discover how adults react to pointing in different contexts and thus become aware of the various usages of pointing. Based on this theory, pointing is not primarily social, but part of a child's early behavioral repertoire that gains social functions through activities involving pointing actions. Consequently, the communicative insight shown by infants when they point does not have an innate basis, but emerges as the result of social interaction. This theory is supported by the fact that infants often point when they are alone and do not always seem to care whether others follow their points. Toddlers who are alone seem to point at things they try to remember, using *private pointing* analogous to the function of **private speech** in problem solving (see Book 4, *Cognition, Intelligence and Learning*, Chapter 19) (Delgado et al., 2011). These examples demonstrate how pointing changes throughout the first year of life and gradually emerges as a social and referential tool. The notion of physical exploration as a basis for pointing can furthermore contribute to an understanding of joint attention and communicative development in blind children, whose early proximal pointing involves physical touch (von Tetzchner and Sedberg, 2005).

Symbolic Gestures

Symbolic gestures are characterized by the fact that they can be translated by a word, such as when a child shakes her head to say "no," flaps her arms for "bird," or turns her hand in a locking movement for "key." Hence, their use is more specific and less dependent on the immediate situation than pointing, which merely indicates a direction. Children usually but not always begin to point before they say their first words (McGillion et al., 2017), while symbolic gestures appear around the same time as the first words, and occasionally a little earlier (Petitto, 1992). However, some children with severe language and communication disorders find it easier to learn symbolic gestures and signs than speech (Lederer and Battaglia, 2015) (see also Chapter 11).

The use of symbolic gestures increases after the age of 2 years, once children have begun to understand what words can be used for and their vocabulary begins to grow. Goldin-Meadow (2015) found that many early gestures are associated with objects and reflect their physical properties (iconicity). She believes children use symbolic gestures not as "labels" in the way words are used, but to describe a visual property of an object when they lack the word. Iconic gestures conveying actions come later, often long after the child has begun to use the word associated with the gesture, and serve as supple mental descriptions to spoken words. In an **experiment** with 18- and 26-month-olds who were taught new spoken words and gestures, both groups learned the words, but only the youngest children learned the gestures (Namy and Waxman, 1998). The older children thus did not seem to accept that a gesture can have the equivalent status of a word.

Symbolic gestures vary from **culture** to culture (Morris et al., 1979). Therefore it is likely that children primarily learn symbolic gestures from observing their parents and other adults (Tomasello and Camaioni, 1997). Children sometimes make their own gestures when they lack words, and some child gestures are not commonly used by adults. In addition, some of the child's hand movements may have been over interpreted by the adult and assigned a meaning that in turn has been adopted by the child. These types of idiosyncratic gestures are comparable to *vocables* (see Chapter 6).

Animal Gestures

Many species use communicative expressions to relay information about food, danger and the like (Håkansson and Westander, 2013). Dogs, dolphins, apes and many other species can also be trained to obey human gestures and spoken words (Herman, 2010). The chimpanzee Nim Chimpsky (named after Noam Chomsky), for example, learned 125 signs in the course of 4 years of training (Terrace, 1979). Other studies have shown that apes are capable of using non-vocal communication systems, but even with extensive training, communication remains extremely limited compared with human language (see Herrmann et al., 2007; Håkansson and Westander, 2013). This underlines the biological foundation of human communication.

6

The Development of Language

Three important characteristics distinguish human language from the communicative expressions of other species: It consists of linguistic *symbols* that represent social conventions to draw attention to specific people, things, events and ideas. It has **grammar**, which allows the symbols to be arranged in patterns according to certain conventions – *sentence structures* – that create meaning beyond the individual symbols themselves. And thirdly, more than 6,000 different human languages exist, while other species mostly have one small common set of communicative expressions (Tomasello, 2006). This implies that humans have a very different and more flexible basis for communication development than other species.

Spoken language includes a system of speech sounds (**phonology**), an inventory of words (vocabulary), a grammar that governs word order (**syntax**) and inflection (**morphology**), and different areas of application (**pragmatics**). **Sign language** incorporates the same features, but here the hands take over the function of the speech organs (see Chapter 11).

Main Theories

No generally accepted "standard theory" of language development exists. Instead, many theories abound, and there is considerable disagreement about the biological basis and the underlying mechanisms of how children develop grammatical competence. Following is a brief presentation of the most important theories that also shows the range of different viewpoints, and a discussion of their status.

DOI: 10.4324/9781003292524-6

Nativism

Nativism represents one theoretical extreme in that it considers language to be based on innate linguistic knowledge, facilitated by a language **module** in the brain specialized to perceive language stimulation (see Book 4, *Cognition, Intelligence and Learning*, Chapter 2). According to Chomsky (1986), the language module contains a **language acquisition device** (LAD) that enables children to divide the flow of speech and identify word classes and grammatical categories in the language or languages they grow up with. The language module has been shaped by evolution and its function is predetermined, just like the function of the heart, liver, and other organs. Pinker (1994) calls it the "language instinct," much like the spider's **instinct** for spinning a web.

The fact that children learn the language that surrounds them is in itself evidence that experience determines the type of language a child acquires, but according to Chomsky (1968, 2000), these are merely "surface differences." The "deep structure" of language that all sentences are derived from places such tight **constraints** on how the human brain can perceive and process linguistic stimulation, that all languages closely resemble each other from a formal point of view. The language acquisition device includes a **universal grammar** with a limited set of options for each existing grammatical aspect or "parameter," for example whether language expresses a spatial relationship such as "in" or "on" as a preposition (preceding nouns and verbs), postposition (following nouns and verbs) or an inflection of a noun or a verb. It thus limits the possible functions of specific words and parts of words in a sentence.

The main nativistic argument for innateness of linguistic structure is "the poverty of the stimulus." The claim is that the language children are exposed to is too impoverished to provide the necessary basis for forming the grammatical rules that competent language users must know. Universal grammar enables children to learn a language with all its complexities from a minimal language input. Similar to how the eye perceives different colors, the child perceives some words as the subject of a statement, others as adjectival, and so on. As long as a child is exposed to language, the universal grammar will quickly establish a grammar in the child with the properties of the language in the surroundings. The universal grammar thus also determines the kind of language a child can learn: human beings are incapable of developing a language not specified by universal grammar (Jackend-off, 2002; Wexler, 1999; Wunderlich, 2004).

Behaviorism

Behaviorism represents another theoretical extreme. It completely rejects the notion of language acquisition as genetically determined, modular knowledge. In "Verbal behavior," Skinner (1957) explains the acquisition of language with the same basic learning mechanisms as any other type of behavior: **conditioning, reinforcement** and **imitation** (see Book 1, *Theoretical Perspectives and Methodology*, Chapter 12). This position is maintained by more recent behaviorists (Greer and Keohane, 2005; Novak and Peláez, 2004). *Relational frame theory* is an extension of Skinner's descriptions and theoretical explanations which retains the basic mechanisms suggested of his theory and also includes processes like analogical reasoning (see Book 4, *Cognition, Intelligence and Learning*, Chapter 15) and perspective taking (see Book 4, *Cognition, Intelligence and Learning*, Chapter 18) (Barnes-Holmes et al., 2001).

Social Constructivism

The central claim of *social constructivist theories* (see Book 1, *Theoretical Perspectives and Methodology*, Chapter 14) is that language is a **cultural tool** that cannot be created by children on their own but must be learned through others (Lisina, 1985; Vygotsky, 1962). According to Bruner (1975, 1983), the use of words and structure of language is learned through social interaction with more competent children and adults. His response to Chomsky's ideas is that children need a **language acquisition support system** (LASS) in order for any supposed language acquisition device (LAD) to function. The support system is not a form of "training," but a scaffold that takes place in the context of social activities in which children and adults participate together, often involving everyday routines and other activities that recur with some variation. Language development is guided through these interactions (Lock, 1980; Thorne and Tasker, 2011).

Emergentism

Emergentism has its basis in cognitive development, including Piaget's theory and **information processing**, and **connectionism** in particular (MacWhinney and O'Grady, 2015). Language is not rooted in a specific linguistic mechanism, but gradually emerges as the result of interaction between *general* cognitive mechanisms and linguistic experience (Karmiloff-Smith, 2011; MacWhinney, 2015). Then there is no need for any language acquisition device or universal grammar. Contrary to Chomsky, emergentism considers the language environment to be "rich" enough to provide sufficient information to allow children to learn a language. By using computer simulations, connectionists have demonstrated that it is possible for a computer − a far simpler device than the human brain − to learn grammatical rules based on the equivalent experiences a child would have (Elman et al., 1996; Vogt and Lieven, 2010).

Usage-based Theory

The usage-based theory of Tomasello (2003, 2009) belongs to the tradition of functionalism. It is closely related to social constructivism in its stress on the importance of **social mediation** and co-construction, while at the same time emphasizing general cognitive processes and children's ability to recognize the perceptual and social patterns of linguistic stimulation. Children learn language from the language they hear (or see) and by communicating and using language for different reasons and in different contexts. The regularities of grammar arise from these experiences. This is how the theory is "usage-based." According to usage-based theory children have an innate basis for communication that manifests itself in the human propensity for community and cooperation. The developmental trajectory is determined by the child's experiences in situations involving communication and language, allowing room for individual developmental variation (Lieven, 2014, 2016).

Theoretical Status

There are many good descriptions of **typical development** and of some of the variation in typical and atypical acquisition of spoken language and sign language. Based on current knowledge, it is nevertheless impossible to determine which theories provide the most accurate description of language development.

Nativism has always had a strong standing among theories of language development and is the most established theory from a historic point of view. It was long believed that children would develop spoken language even if they were not exposed to language (O'Neill, 1980). One main criticism of nativism is that language does not develop but is "prefabricated." Children are learning language by activating an innate grammar – all a child needs is a modicum of exposure to language, analogous to making coffee by pouring hot water into a cup filled with instant coffee. But language is not an instinct: instinctive behavior is generally quite stereotyped and appears even if an animal grows up isolated from the normal experiences of the species. This does not apply to language (Evans, 2014; Tomasello, 1995).

The fact that the human species alone has language supports the likelihood of a unique human biological predisposition for developing language. However, this need not be a universal grammar or any other specifically linguistic feature (Tomasello, 2005). It may just as well be a neurological structure with significance for human **perception**, **cognition** and **learning** in general. The argument that language is too complex to be learned without detailed genetically determined knowledge does not seem to be valid (Braine, 1994; Tomasello, 2003, 2005). Not only has human language evolved too recently for evolution to select genes that ensure the development of a detailed mechanism such as universal grammar, but the human brain and body must also be able to produce the communicative expressions that develop into language. It is therefore more likely that communicative expressions reflect the human brain and body, rather than being the result of an evolutionary neurological **adaptation** to a language environment that did not yet exist (Christiansen and Chater, 2008). However, in spite of considerable criticism, nativism has maintained a solid position in language development.

The behavioristic account of language development (Skinner, 1957) met with considerable opposition from the outset (Chomsky, 1959), and behaviorism has exerted little influence on contemporary research into children's language. Critics maintain that conditioning and imitation are inadequate mechanisms to explain the development of language, and that behavioral explanations ignore the meaning of language. Inhelder and Piaget (1964) point out that if language learning merely involved conditioning, children would start to learn language in their second month of life. Children are rarely corrected in their use of language and construct many sentences they have never heard before, such as *ball up* or *there boy*. Neither do children's errors suggest that they simply imitate. Instead, they acquire a language system that may be described as a set of grammatical constructions. This is evident in children's overgeneralizations of such constructions, such as when they say *goed* instead of *went* during a certain period. In view of this unanimous criticism, it is difficult to understand why language instruction for children with autism spectrum disorders, **intellectual disability** and other severe **developmental disorders** is often based on Skinner's ideas in applied behavior analysis (see Bondy and Frost, 2002; Durand and Merges, 2001; Mirenda, 1997).

Most developmental theorists of the twenty-first century position themselves somewhere between nature and nurture in regard to the development of language. They believe that human genes allow language to be acquired via cognitive and social functions, but without a genetic linguistic basis in the way proposed by Chomsky and Pinker. *Functionalism* has a long history of challenging the nativist view of language development, and Tomasello's usage-based theory is the most important non–nativist theory today. Based on a large number of studies, Tomasello (2003, 2009) and others have shown that the acquisition of vocabulary and grammar can be explained by children's social and cognitive skills and interactions with more competent children and adults. According to Tomasello, it is children's understanding of intention that provides the innate decisive element in language development, from the earliest communicative efforts to the development of grammar.

By using computer simulations of the language learning process, *connectionists* have demonstrated that language learning does not need to depend on genetically specified categories (Chang et al., 2006). Connectionism argues that children are able to analyze sensory stimulation and that their overall learning capacity is sufficient to detect regularities in the language from what they hear or see in their environment (Elman et al., 1996; Westermann et al., 2009). A certain innate basis remains nonetheless. Some theorists maintain that children have an innate sensitivity to probability structure – an awareness of things that often occur together, that allows them to discover linguistic regularities (Erickson and Thiessen, 2015). At the same time, theories based on *information processing* are met with the objection that language development cannot be explained based exclusively on the processing of information, independent of other human factors. Such processes must incorporate meaning and direction, and can therefore only be understood within a social context (Campbell, 1986; Nelson, 2007a).

Karmiloff-Smith (2005) argues that Bruner (1983) and other social constructivists place too much emphasis on social interaction and too little on cognitive processes. She and Bruner represent the two basic twenty-first-century perspectives on what language development is about. Karmiloff-Smith focuses mainly on neurology and the underlying cognitive processes, as well as on the "technical" aspects of language: its conceptual foundation, the structure of vocabulary and the rules of grammar. Bruner emphasizes the social cognitive basis of language, its pragmatic aspects and its function in social interaction. The *emergentist coalition model* is one of several theories attempting to reconcile these two perspectives. According to this model, language development has its origins in purely perceptual and associative processes, followed by linguistic and social processes that furnish the basis for word use and sentence structure (Hollich et al., 2000; Parish-Morris et al., 2013).

The Emergence of Speech

During the first months of life, the infant's sounds consist of crying and cooing. Children usually begin to babble around the age of 6 months, but here, too, there is considerable variation. Since infants with profound deafness vocalize as well, their sound production cannot be used as an early clue to normal hearing. **Babbling**, however, is delayed in deaf children and is somewhat different in quantity as well as quality from the babbling sounds of children with normal hearing, and babbling may not appear without a cochlear implant (see Book 3, *Perceptual and Motor Development*, Chapter 4) (Fagan, 2015).

Initially, the babbling sounds of hearing children consist of series of identical consonant-vowel syllables, for example *dadadada* or *nanana*. Gradually, these sounds become more varied and incorporate several different consonants into the same sound sequence. Additional sounds include pure vowel sequences, vowel-consonant sequences and consonant-vowel-consonant sequences. Accentuation patterns and **intonation** contours become more differentiated, and gradually render the production of sound more varied and similar to speech. Children with early onset of babbling also tend to say their first words early (McGillion et al., 2017).

Early babbling is identical across languages, but around the age of 10 months it begins to absorb the sound of the surrounding language, for example whether the child grows up in a French, Swedish, English or Japanese language environment (Vihman, 1993). During the babbling phase, children also "play" with speech sounds and practice pronouncing the sounds they have heard (Kuczaj, 1982).

Studies have found that deaf infants who are exposed to early sign language produce hand movements with hand shapes that do not constitute manual signs but have the same similarity to the hand movements and shapes found in sign language as babbling has to speech. This kind of manual activity, which they call *grabling*, is not found in hearing children (Petitto and Marentette, 1991).

Perception of Speech Sounds

Every language has its own unique set of speech sounds, or **phonemes**, the smallest sound units that distinguish words with different meanings. /M/ and /p/ belong to different phonemes because *mark* and *park* are different words. The number of phonemes in a language vary from 12 to just under 100. On a global scale, about 600 consonants and 200 vowels are in use (Ladefoged, 2004). Many animals communicate by using sounds, but none of them with a system that corresponds to human phonemes (Collier et al., 2014).

All children with normal hearing share the same basis for perceiving speech sounds, and must learn to differentiate, recognize and produce exactly those speech sounds that distinguish meaning in the language or languages they grow up with. In English, /r/ and /l/ belong to different phonemes. Japanese and Chinese speakers have great difficulty distinguishing between /r/ and /l/ because they belong to the same phoneme and thus do not yield different words in Japanese or Chinese. Therefore, many Chinese speakers say *low* instead of *row*, or *lice* instead of *rice*. A child of Japanese origin growing up in an English-speaking environment usually has no trouble detecting the difference between /l/ and /r/ or other sounds that differentiate the meaning of English words. Very early in development, infants are able to distinguish most speech sounds, regardless of language. Box 6.1 shows a typical experiment examining the ability of infants to distinguish between speech sounds (see also Book 3, *Perceptual and Motor Development*, Chapter 4).

Young infants are capable of discriminating between speech sounds that do not change the meaning of a word in their own language, but later find it difficult to distinguish between these sounds. Two- to 3-month-old Japanese children, for example, are able to tell the

Box 6.1   Early Discrimination of Speech Sounds (based on Eimas, 1985, p. 47)

Four-month-old infants were exposed to a speech sound such as *ba* or *pa* from a loudspeaker whenever they sucked on a pacifier. The speech sound was interesting to the infants and made them suck more. After listening to the same sound repeatedly, the infants lost interest and their sucking slowed (**habituation**). Some of the infants continued to hear the same sound while others heard a new sound. After 5 minutes, the sucking rate had decreased significantly and kept declining among those infants who continued to hear the same sounds. Infants who were exposed to a different speech sound showed an increase in their sucking rate instead (**dishabituation**). By using this method, it has been possible to show that infants at this age are able to hear the difference between *ba* and *pa*, *ba* and *ma*, and other phonemic contrasts.

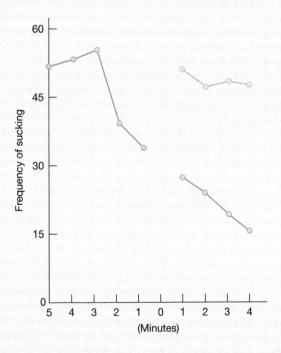

difference between /l/ and /r/ just like infants of the same age in other language cultures (Kuhl, 1992).

The actual perception of phonemes only occurs once the sounds are incorporated into a meaningful context, that is, once children learn that different sound combinations have unique meanings and functions, for example that the sound *Teddy* refers to a dog and *Siam* to a cat. As children's vocabulary increases, the acoustic differences between the words they learn are perceived as being worthy of attention, while differences that do not give rise to different words are perceived as carrying no meaning and eventually are no longer differentiated. Since it would interfere with children's understanding of language if they were to notice differences between speech sounds that did not also involve a difference in meaning, children actively ignore them. At the same time, children become more sensitive to the differences between sounds that result in different meanings (Maurer and Werker, 2014). In this way, **recognition** gradually becomes more enculturated and adapted to the language or languages in the child's surroundings (Kuhl, 1993; Werker, 1991). Studies have shown that infants exhibit differences in brain activation when they hear their own language compared with the sounds of languages they have never experienced before (Kuhl, 2010).

During the first years of life, children comprehend a fast-growing number of words. Consequently, the ability to recognize sequences of speech sounds is well enough developed in most children not to impose significant constraints on the acquisition of words. With increasing age, children also improve at recognizing new words even if they are pronounced somewhat differently than when they first heard the word (McQueen et al., 2012).

Production of Speech

Many of the first words uttered by children resemble babbling sounds, such as *mama* and *papa* (Lewis, 1936). Children continue to babble for some time after producing their first words, and it is not always easy to hear whether an infant is babbling or attempting to say a word, and what the intended word may be. Since many common words resemble babbling sounds, adults may interpret these sounds as acoustically similar words that make sense in a given situation (Bjerkan et al., 1983). At the same time, children begin to produce simple sound combinations – **vocables** – that are not found in the language spoken by adults (Ferguson, 1978). The first words children utter are therefore not always a direct copy of what they hear. Children are highly creative in how they acquire language and invent their own vocables early on while trying to find out what different words can be used for. The very existence of vocables emphasizes the gradual transition from babbling to adult-like speech, and from prelinguistic to linguistic communication.

The ability to articulate speech sounds develops gradually. Words require rapid and complex motor movements that take time to learn. /b/, /d/ and /m/ are mastered early, while /r/ is one of the last sounds acquired by English-speaking children and can pose challenges all the way until **school age** (McLeod and Bleile, 2003). During their first years, many children simplify the articulation of many words, for example by saying *tootie* for *cookie*, or *dod* for *dog*. As children learn more words, their repertoire of sounds increases, but during early development children are often selective and choose words they are able to pronounce (Clark, 2016). It takes time to develop an awareness of the sounds words are composed of and the differences between them, an insight children often gain in connection with learning how to read.

Perception and Production of Speech

Although perception and use of speech are related, they can develop in slightly different ways. Children can perceive acoustic differences they themselves are not yet capable of producing. As a rule, the more articulation errors children make, the greater their problems perceiving the differences between words, although many children are able to differentiate words despite not being able to articulate them differently when they speak (Strange and Broen, 1980). Hence, the relationship between perception and production can vary from one child to the next.

A developmental trend is the gradual reduction in children's ability to hear the difference between what they themselves say and what others are saying. They can hear the articulation errors of others without being aware that they themselves say the same words incorrectly, such as in the following example in which a father and his son are watching ships in the harbor (MacWhinney, 2015, p. 306):

Child: *Look at this big sip.*
Father: *Yes, it is quite a big sip.*
Child: *No, Daddy, say "sip" not "sip."*

Although the boy said "sip," he thought he had said "ship," which is what it sounded like to him. Had he heard what he actually said on a recording, he would probably have realized that his own articulation was wrong. Another study found that 3-year-olds perceived words spoken by adults better than the same words spoken by themselves on a recording. The more their own articulation deviated from that of the adult, the more difficult it was for the children to understand the words (Dodd, 1975).

The difficulties involved in hearing one's own articulation cause problems in connection with learning to pronounce foreign languages. Because over time children increasingly lose the ability to correct their own articulation, infants born with a cleft lip or palate receive surgery in the first few months of life to allow them as much time as possible to take advantage of this ability (Kuehn and Moller, 2000).

Early Word Learning

The transition from prelinguistic to linguistic communication takes place once the child begins to understand and apply words to communicate about people, animals, objects, actions, events, and so on. Children must be able to infer a word's *reference*, based on their knowledge and their perception of the situation. They must be able to understand whether the word represents the name of something that is or is not present in the environment, whether it refers to something to do with the child itself or with something else, and so on. Besides, word learning is about far more than linking a word form to a conceptual category. Children must understand the relevant communicative action, the intent behind the words others say, such as why they name something or comment on an event or a characteristic. The phrase "it's hot" entails completely different meanings depending on whether it refers to the weather or to a bowl of soup (Brown, 1958; Tomasello, 2003).

The First Words

Children comprehend words before they themselves begin to use words in a way others can understand. Saying a word demands more of a child than merely showing an understanding of it. In investigations of word comprehension, the child usually has to point at something or react in another meaningful way when a word is spoken. Studies of language use require children to activate and produce a word, as well as to show an underlying intention. Imitation is not enough – children imitate many words they do not understand. Additionally, it is difficult to assess children's partial comprehension of words while they are still progressing to a more mature understanding. It is easier to register how children use words. This may be one reason why comprehension has been far less studied than usage, and why knowledge remains quite limited (Bishop, 2006).

Children usually say their first words around the age of 1, but with major variation. Some children are 9 months, while others begin at 17 months or later. Girls generally begin to speak slightly earlier than boys. In one study, parents registered that their children had used an average of ten words by the age of 13 months, and 50 words 3 months later, but 10 percent of the children had used fewer than five words at 16 months (see Figure 6.2). By the age of 2 years, the average lies at around 150 words, and children can have learned anywhere from 10 to 450 words (MacWhinney, 2015). Nelson (1988) describes three periods in the early development of words (Box 6.2).

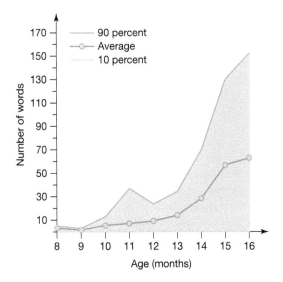

Figure 6.1 Early vocabulary.

The blue line shows the average vocabulary size and number of words of 8–16-month-old children, based on a **checklist** filled out by their parents. The red line shows the boundary for the 90th percentile (based on Bates et al., 1995, p. 103).

Box 6.2   Three Periods in Early *Lexical Development* (from Nelson, 1988)

The acquisition of words is characterized by periods posing different challenges.

Period 1

The child faces the problem of finding a way into the language system: understanding what words are, what they refer to, and what they can be used for. This period begins once children first become sensitive to language forms and consistently respond to some of them, and continues until the production of 30 or more words. It usually lasts for 6–12 months, with considerable spread: for some children it begins as early as 9 months, for others it lasts until the age of 2.

Period 2

The start of this period is when children have acquired about 30 words and have a basic knowledge of words and conceptual categories. It is marked by an increase in the rate of acquiring new words (and possibly a vocabulary spurt). By now, children have developed an understanding of what words are and want to know the name of everything they see. Their main challenge is to discover the meaning behind the words they hear and associate the conceptual categories they have formed of people, objects and events in their physical and social world with the corresponding words. During this period, children also seem to assume that a single word corresponds to a single category, and vice versa. It is a two-way process: children try to find the right words for existing categories, and categories for the words they hear. This period lasts several years.

Period 3

The third period generally begins around the age of 3–4 years and is characterized by increasing insight into language. It is a period of revision, reorganization and consolidation of lexical items within domains of related words. There is an increase in the use of previously limited word classes, such as relational terms.

Word learning not only builds on the child's previously acquired concepts, but also encourages the child to form new concepts – a word can act as an invitation to form a category (Brown, 1958; Nelson, 2007a). As early as the beginnings of language development, children perceive toy animals with identical names to belong to the same category, while toy animals with dissimilar names are perceived as being different (Waxman and Braun, 2005; Xu, 2002). Thus, words form a bridge that links together the perception of children and adults about the world and its concepts.

Fast Mapping

The first time children hear a word, they must – without any awareness on their own part – form an assumption about its meaning and use. This first attribution of meaning to a word is called "fast mapping" (Dollaghan, 1985). By fast mapping, the child starts to turn an unknown word into a known one by creating a mental **representation** of the word's form and use, such as *cat* referring to a small four-legged animal. This is necessary in order to recognize the word later and make use of it in other situations. Without this first attribution of meaning, the word would appear to be new every time the child heard it. Sometimes, fast mapping leads to a correct understanding of the word's meaning, but for most early words, fast mapping merely provides the child with a partial clue to begin using the word. The complexity of the sound and the meaning of a new word will influence the fast mapping, and children with language disorders have more difficulties with fast mapping and learning new words than children without language disorders (Alt and Plante, 2006). The process from perceiving a word for the first time to the adult's understanding and nuanced use of it can take a long time (Dollaghan, 1985).

Overextension and Underextension

Many words take time to learn and children's early use of a word can be both broader, narrower and different from that of an adult. The *extension* of a word consists of all the exemplars that pertain to and can be represented by the word. **Overextension** occurs when a word is used beyond its conventional meaning. When my nephew Frederik was 3 years old, he pointed at my cat and enthusiastically said *woof-woof*. For a while he used the same word for cats and dogs (see also Book 4, *Cognition, Intelligence and Learning*, Chapter 14). When Dromi's (1993) daughter Keren was about 16 months old, she used the term *broom* for all items stored in a particular cupboard in the kitchen.

Underextension occurs when words are used in a narrower sense than usual. The word may be correct when it is used but it is not always used when it would be appropriate (Griffiths, 1986). When Keren was between 12 and 15 months, her white toy elephant was the only thing she called *elephant*. She never said *elephant* when playing outside on a small slide with the shape of an elephant, or when her mother showed her pictures of elephants or toy elephants made of plastic. For a certain period, when Keren had gotten a little older, she said *walk* only while walking around the house wearing one of her parents' pair of shoes. She never said *walk* in response to her mother's question about people passing by or when she herself was walking barefoot. Dromi (1993) observed approximately the same number of overextensions and underextensions in her daughter.

Over time, the language environment usually provides children with sufficient clues to correct their own use of words and understanding of the categories particular words refer to. The use of a word is therefore not static, but changes over time. When young children make "errors" these do not reflect an inability to categorize or learn words, but rather the fact that children make use of this ability. The nuanced use of words by older children and adults is the result of long experience with words in different communicative situations.

The Vocabulary Spurt

Acquiring the first words can take time. For children with typical language development it can take up to 5 months from when they utter their first recognizable word until they have used ten words (Harris, M., 1992). Often children use only a few words, as if trying to find out what those words can be used for. This is illustrated in a **diary study** of Jessie's development. From the age of 15 to 20 months, her utterances were dominated by *cat* and *mom*. She said each word over 5,000 times – more than 30 times a day. Between the age of 17 and 20 months, she only used a handful of other words: *hi*, *dad*, *blow*, *apple* and *there* (Labov and Labov, 1978).

Toward the end of the second year of life, the rate of learning new words usually increases. The beginning of what is known as the **vocabulary spurt** is often defined as the first month in which vocabulary increases by at least 15 words (Poulin-Dubois and Graham,

1994). It can occur at different ages: some children show an increase in word learning as early as 13 months of age, while others are 25 months before the vocabulary spurt sets in (Bloom, 1993). However, some children show a more gradual increase in vocabulary rather than a sudden and rapid surge (Bloom, 2004; Reznick and Goldfield, 1992).

The Content of Children's First Words

Children's early vocabulary reflects their cognitive development and knowledge about the world, their interests and preferences, what adults talk about with children, and physical and emotional aspects of the situations they participate in. The names of animals, for example, including exotic animals like alligators and zebras, stand for a relatively large proportion of toddler vocabulary (Gleason et al., 2009). This is related to the interest children often show in animals, but also the fact that Western adults tend to give toddlers picture books about animals.

Children learn the words they hear in their surroundings (or see, in the case of sign language), but word learning is not merely an imitative process. In a study of how a group of children used the first ten words they had learned (40 different words in all), as many as 37 of the words could be traced to how each child's mother had used the word right before. A little later, the children used 29 of the words in a new way, while 11 words were used exactly as before. Seventeen of the 29 new word uses were related to how each child's mother had used the word just moments before the child used it, while 12 of the words were used in ways the children had not heard from their mother, at least not recently (Barrett et al., 1991). This means that children make active use of familiar words for their own communicative purposes even during the earliest language development.

Words are used to talk about many different things. One of the key questions is how children are able to understand what a word used in a given situation refers to. A number of researchers believe this to be such a difficult task, that there must be limitations to the types of assumptions a child can form about the meaning of a word during early language development. Some suggest that children have an innate tendency to assume that words refer to whole objects unless the situation clearly indicates something else, and that this is why object words dominate children's early vocabulary (Golinkoff et al., 1995; Markman, 1992). However, this could just as well reflect adults' tendency to name whole objects when talking to children. Observations show that mothers tend to name whole objects rather than parts

Box 6.3   Language Input: Maternal Labeling of Novel Animals (Masur, 1997)

Ten boys and ten girls aged 10–21 months were observed for 10–15 minutes in farm and zoo play with their mothers. The mothers produced 667 names of animals previously unknown to the children and whose name they had never heard before. Nearly all the first names provided by the mothers labelled the whole animal. Reference to parts before giving the animal name, such as *What's this? A long, long neck*, occurred only three times. Forty-one times, the first name was accompanied by a reference to parts of the animal (e.g., arm, tail) or its characteristics (e.g., color, size), for example *a little dog*. In a further 27 cases, the first naming was immediately followed by a reference, for example, *That's a bird, a bird with a large beak*. In addition, for 51 animals, reference to parts or other characteristics followed two or more statements after the animal had first been named. When all were included in the count, parts of animals or their characteristics were mentioned in 119 of 667 cases.

of objects and characteristics when they introduce new things to toddlers (Masur, 1997). The results in Box 6.3 show that an assumption of innate constraints is unnecessary in explaining toddlers' tendency to learn the names of whole objects; neither is there agreement about the time frame in which any possible constraints may be in effect (Clark, 2016). Adults' use of language is sufficient to allow children to learn many new words for whole objects.

Toddlers spend much of their time exploring objects in the environment and often ask adults about the names of things. However, although they typically first label the whole object, parents and other adults do not simply name the objects children are engaged with, that would quickly become repetitive. They talk about what children do with the objects, such as throwing or kicking a ball, cuddling with a doll, pushing a toy car, and about how objects behave – the ball rolls, the music box plays a melody and the down quilt keeps you warm. They also talk about the characteristics of people, animals, objects and actions, for example that the kitty is cute, the baby is small, the ball is red and the boy runs fast (Nelson, 2007a; Tomasello, 2008). Although object words make up a significant portion of children's vocabulary during the second year of life, they make up less than 50 percent of all words (Bates et al., 1995; Bornstein et al., 2004).

Cultural differences in early vocabulary also support the assumption that the proportion of object words reflects children's language environment. The large number of object words among toddlers in Western countries may reflect that joint activities between children and adults typically include many toys and picture books. Children in Korea and China experience fewer such activities and have a smaller proportion of object words in their early vocabulary compared with children in the USA and Europe. This runs counter to the assumption that vocabulary is determined by an innate tendency to interpret words as the names of whole objects (Gopnik and Choi, 1995; Tardif, 1996, 2006).

The other major category in early vocabulary is made up of action words that refer to what humans and animals do, such as *run*, *cry*, *play*, *wait* or *think*. In a study of 20-month-old children, these made up about 20 percent of all words (Bornstein et al., 2004). Since actions have different durations, they are not always readily perceived as clearly defined units. Children ask adults more often about the names of things rather than the names of actions, although the question *What is she doing?* is not uncommon among toddlers. Also the situations

Box 6.4 Context Guides Children's Understanding of New Words (Tomasello and Akhtar, 1995)

Thirty-six children aged 20–26 months participated in the study. There were two conditions with two objects that were unknown to the children (a small wooden toy that wobbled when rolled or a complex string of blocks with bells inside) and two novel actions (throwing the object down a chute or shooting it out with a "catapult"). In both conditions, the experimenter was sitting together with the child. With 12 of the children, the experimenter first threw several familiar objects down the chute or shot them out with the catapult, and then said *modi* when doing the action with the new object. With 12 other children, the experimenter carried out a number of familiar play actions with the object before saying *modi* and performing the new play action. A **control group** of 12 children (six in each condition) went through the same procedures but the experimenter said only *Watch!* or *Look there!* and *modi* was not mentioned until they were asked the test question (below).

Somewhat later, the experimenter and the child sat down together with all the objects used in the two situations. The experimenter said to the child: *Look over there. Can you show me modi?* Seven of the 12 children who had taken part in the situation with the chute took the object and showed it to the experimenter, implying that they had perceived *modi* as the name of the object. Nine of the 12 children who had been involved in the situation with different play actions performed the new action they had observed, and thus seemed to have perceived *modi* as the name of the action. One of the children in the control group performed the new action when asked to modi. Two in each **experimental group** and 11 children in the control group made other responses.

The results indicate that the children perceived the new word as the label of what was new in the situation. In the first situation, the object was new, in the second situation the action.

associated with objects words and action words differ to some degree. Mothers use more object words when looking at a picture book together with their child, and more verbs when playing with toys (Altınkamışet al., 2014). In addition, children use various situational cues to determine whether a word refers to an object or an action (Box 6.4). Toddlers tend to associate unknown words with what is new in the situation.

Children's early vocabulary also contains some words that refer to characteristics and qualities such as shape, color, temperature, size, height and kindness. At 20 months, these words make up about one-tenth of children's vocabulary (Bornstein et al., 2004). *Function words* include words that express relationships between objects, people, places and events, such as the prepositions *in* and *on*. Unlike many objects and to some extent action words, they cannot be pointed at or physically differentiated, and their acquisition is more related to sentence formation (Thorseng, 1997).

Individual Styles

Although people share a common language, the development of language is individual. *Mama* and *papa* are not always among the first ten words (Tardif et al., 2008). Nelson (1973) found that some children had more than 25 object words among their first 50 words. For other children, first names and social words and phrases such as *please, hi, stop, yes, no* and *ouch* made up the largest share. Nelson suggested that the differences in word use have their origin in different cognitive styles and the way in which children organize their experiences, and that children at this age have different "theories" about how language is used. The first group she calls **referential**, since most of children's words referred to objects. The second group she calls *expressive*, meaning that children in this group used more words referring to social situations and their own experiences. Children in the expressive group seemed to perceive language more as a tool for social interaction, while the referential group mostly used language to communicate about things in the environment. Both groups showed typical development and the study illustrates that there is more than one way to language competence (Nelson, 1981).

The Contrast Principle

In a certain sense, an infant's first words consist of isolated units, while words acquired later also take on meaning because they are different from words already contained in the vocabulary (de Saussure, 1974). According to Clark (1992), word learning follows the *principle of contrast*, meaning that a difference in form always entails a difference in meaning. Children assume that every new word has a meaning different from the words they have previously learned. The discovery that two or more words can be *synonyms* with roughly the same meaning comes relatively late, according to Clark. Yet, studies have shown that toddlers both perceive and use new words about objects whose names they already know (Gathercole, 1987; Merriman, 1986). Nelson (1988), on the other hand, suggests that children first begin to use the principle of contrast later in **childhood** as the result of word learning, rather than as one of its requirements. Adults often use contrasting terms when explaining the meaning of a word to children, for example, that one car is *big* and another *small*, or that something is *above* and something else *below* a bridge (Clark, 2016).

Further Growth in Vocabulary

Both toddlers and older children spend much of their time talking. Not only do children learn how to speak, they also speak in order to learn. By using wireless microphones attached to children's clothing, Wagner (1985) registered all the words spoken by seven children aged 1½–9 years in the course of one day. The youngest child used 1,860 different words for a total of 13,800 words. The most talkative child that day used 37,700 words (Table 16.1).

Following the vocabulary spurt, or alternately a more gradual growth in vocabulary, word learning increases at a formidable pace. Estimates vary anywhere from an average of 5.5 to 9 words per day until the age of 18 years. Around 6 years of age, children are usually able to comprehend between 10,000 and 15,000 words, and produce somewhat fewer (Anglin, 1993; Carey, 1978). Both the situation and the linguistic context provide guidelines for the possible interpretation of words, such as the meaning of *helicopter* when the child's mother says *The helicopter makes a lot of noise* when something is flying past. The word's placement in the sentence and the adult's inflection of it are important clues to the type of word that may be involved, for example

Table 6.1 Children's word production in the course of one day (the number of different words and the total number of words used in the course of one day by seven German children aged 1;5–9;7 years (Wagner, 1985))

	Age (years;months)	Total number of word forms	Number of different word forms
Katrin	1;5	13,800	1,860
Andreas	2;5	20,200	2,210
Carsten	3;6	37,700	4,790
Gabi	5;4	30,600	2,490
Fredrik	8;7	24,700	4,960
Roman	9;2	24,400	3,860
Teresa	9;7	25,200	3,520

whether it is a noun, a verb or an adjective (Nagy and Townsend, 2012; Snow, 2010).

As children grow older, their conversations increase in length and complexity. They learn the entire range of different word classes and their word use becomes more diverse and flexible. Adolescents improve at varying words, use more words to refer to the same thing, understand that the same word can be used in many different contexts, and that it has a number of different meanings, including its figurative use (see below). School is an important source for new words, and the child's vocabulary is an important tool in academic learning (Nagy and Townsend, 2012). Printed school English consists of approximately 88,500 distinct words, but few children understand all of them (Nagy and Anderson, 1984). It is estimated that English-speaking children learn between 3,000 and 5,400 words a year during primary and secondary school (Berman, 2007). In the course of 12 years of school, this adds up to anywhere between 36,000 and 64,800 words. This shows the tremendous capacity of children and adolescents to learn new words and the complexity of the knowledge they acquire, but also the enormous vocabulary requirements in school.

Figurative Language

Figurative language refers to words that are used in a nonliteral or indirect way, including **metaphors**, similes, irony and humor.

Metaphors often incorporate knowledge from one area in order to understand new areas (Rakova, 2003). Modern examples of linguistic innovation based on metaphor is the word "memory" in connection with computers, or "surfing" on the Internet. Metaphor is a key element in later language development. Although preschoolers occasionally use metaphors spontaneously, for example by saying that *gasoline is milk for the car*, the development of metaphors has barely begun by the time a child starts in school (Levorato and Cacciari, 2002; Nippold, 1998). Children use words in innovative nonliterate ways when they have difficulty retrieving a known word form, like *pourer* for cup or *sleeper* for bed (Clark, 1981). Keil (1986) describes four stages in children's perception of metaphors (Table 16.2). During early development, metaphors are interpreted *literally* rather than *figuratively*. When asked to explain the statement *My sister is a rock*, the 6-year-olds said things like, *She is hard, like if you felt her hand, you couldn't squish it or anything*, or *She just sits there without moving*. The 8-year-olds realized that the statements had to do with behavioral characteristics, and answered that the sister did not give up. The 10-year-olds tended to interpret it as a psychological trait, answering that the sister was mean. However, it is not until 11 or 12 years of age that children are able to formulate the relationship between a hard thing and a hard person

Table 6.2 Children pass through four levels in their comprehension of metaphors involving **personality traits** (based on Keil, 1986)

Level 1	Children take metaphors literally. A "smooth person" is described as someone who has just shaved.
Level 2	Children realize that the statement relates to two areas, both physical and psychological, but fail to juxtapose them. "The idea bloomed" is explained by saying that "it went away."
Level 3	Children juxtapose the two domains along basic inferred dimensions. A "sour person" is someone who is "not very nice," while a "smooth person" is someone who is thoughtful.
Level 4	Children are able to identify the interaction between different domains and interpret the statements correctly. A "sour person" is someone who "doesn't want to do things," a "smooth person" is someone who "takes things without yelling or jumping at people," and an "idea that wasn't ripe yet" is an idea that needed "some more planning."

in the sense that "both a hard thing and a hard person are difficult to handle" (Asch and Nerlove, 1960). In the transition to **adolescence** there is a change in the quantity and quality of figurative language, which may be related to the general increase in knowledge and development of more complex metalinguistic abilities. Adolescents are also better at constructing new figurative expressions (Levorato and Cacciari, 2002; Nippold, 1998).

The studies previously mentioned show that metaphor comprehension is not simply a matter of experience, but also of children's depth of understanding. Although children in early school age have ample experience with both people and things that are hot, cold, smooth and hard, they have difficulty understanding the relationship between personal characteristics and physical expressions. The complex nature of figurative language is also reflected in the challenges experienced by children and adolescents with language impairments (Abrahamsen and Smith, 2000; Kerbel and Grunwell, 1998a, b) and autism spectrum disorder (Happé, 1995). They seem to have difficulty integrating linguistic, social and contextual elements and infer the intended meaning, and the difference between adults is more pronounced than between older children with and without autism – also children without autism struggle with metaphorical language (Chahboun et al., 2016).

Teachers use metaphors to explain scientific concepts and other subjects to students; teaching without metaphors is nearly impossible to imagine (Aubusson et al., 2006; Pramling, 2015). Unfamiliar metaphors can make textbooks inaccessible to children, especially if they struggle with comprehension. At the same time, studies show that children develop a better understanding and usage from texts containing metaphors than from similar texts without metaphors (Winner, 1988). This shows the importance of metaphors in acquiring knowledge and underlines the fact that metaphors in a text (and in language in general) must be designed so children can actually understand them.

Cultural Differences in Word Extension

Languages differ greatly with regard to word extension, that is, the extent of what a word can encompass. This often becomes apparent when translating from one language to another – even actions such as cutting or breaking are not necessarily assigned to the same categories in different languages (Majid et al., 2008).

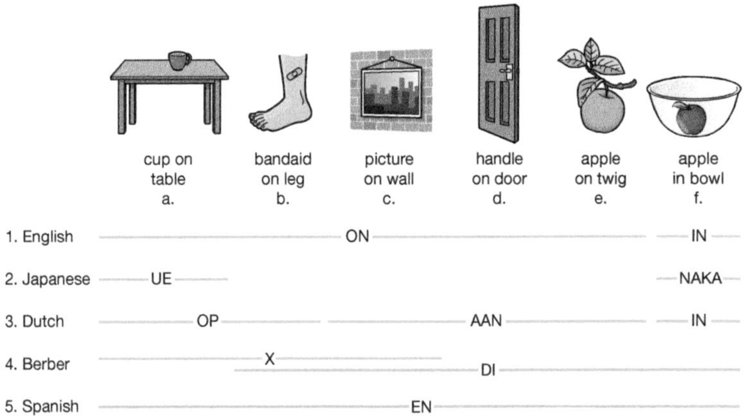

Figure 6.2 Spatial relationships in various languages.

English, Japanese, Dutch, Berber and Spanish speakers refer to the spatial relationships shown in illustrations a–f. 1) In English, Norwegian, Hungarian and several other languages, a, b, c, d and e are *on*, while f is *in*. 2) Japanese uses an unspecified generic term that simply indicates the presence of some spatial relationship that applies to all the illustrations; *ue* (a) is a noun that can be translated as "upper region" or "top," while *naka* (f) can be translated as "inner space." 3) Dutch uses three prepositions: *op* for a and b, *aan* for c, d and e, and *in* for f. 4) Berber uses the preposition *x* for a and *di* for d, e and f. Both can be used for b and c. 5) Spanish uses the same preposition *en* for all the illustrations (based on Bowerman and Choi, 2001).

The differences between languages offer important insights into the development of language, as they reveal the relationship between basic human concepts and words. For example, there is no universal correspondence between the characteristics of physical space and the words that describe these properties. Different cultures not only use dissimilar words, but also divide the world in different ways (Lakoff, 1987). Figure 6.4 shows five ways in which various languages indicate spatial relationships represented by *in* and *on* in English. This means that children who grow up with different languages both use different words when they describe identical spatial relationships and describe different spatial relationships (Bowerman and Choi, 2001; Gentner and Bowerman, 2009).

Expanding Social Activities

The gradual expansion of children's language environment affects their vocabulary. Kindergarten usually represents a broader and more varied language environment than the home. The school introduces many new words, at the same time, as it creates the need for new words. The vocabulary learned at school is a basis for gaining access to education, employment and the general public debate in newspapers and other media. Another part of children's vocabulary comes from magazines and books. Adolescence is marked by a major change in interests and activities. Adolescents spend a lot of time talking together, and their language is typically characterized by many new words and expressions. The variation in children's activities leads to individual differences in word learning, and there is a clear relationship between social background and vocabulary (Hoff, 2013). Culture, too, has an impact on word learning. To some extent, children in Great Britain and the USA talk about other things than children in Uganda and Japan. In adulthood, the growth in vocabulary diminishes. This is partly the result of word learning itself – many words have already been learned – but also of the fact that individual activity patterns become more stable with age.

From Single Words to Sentences

The ability to express an infinite number of different meanings by combining words is the very essence of human language. The transition from single to multi-word utterances is the most important qualitative milestone in language development. Once children begin to combine two or more words, they are able to communicate more specific and complex messages.

Early Understanding of Multi-word Utterances

Children show understanding of multi-word utterances before they themselves begin to use them. Many children who mostly use single-word utterances will perform instructions such as *kiss teddy* and *teddy kiss* in different ways (Sachs and Truswell, 1978). Although children's earliest sentences are typically incomplete and in "telegram style," their comprehension is best when adults use short but complete sentences (Petretic and Tweney, 1977). Toddlers generally do not understand sentences with several embedded clauses (Clark, 2016).

To interpret what they hear, young children use both their language skills and their general knowledge about the world. The study in Box 6.5 shows that from 3 to 5 years, children increasingly relied on sentence structure when inferring meaning from sentences (Strohner and Nelson, 1974). However, children's interpretations can be influenced by inducing a particular perspective. In a similar study, most of a group of 3–4-year-olds let the cat bite the duck when they carried

Box 6.5   Event Probability and Sentence Structure in Young Children's Interpretation of Sentences (Strohner and Nelson, 1974)

Children aged 3 to 5 years (15 in each age group) were asked to act out sentences that were active or passive, and describing probable or improbable events. There were an actor and an object or a recipient in each sentence, and the children had two dolls for each sentence they should act out. The figure shows that all the children correctly acted out active and probable sentences like *The boy throws the ball* without problems. The 3-year-olds had problems with acting out all the sentences describing improbable events. They let the tiger bite the turtle when acting out *The turtle bites the tiger*, seemingly basing their interpretation on what they knew about turtles and tigers. The 4-year-olds correctly acted out most of the active sentences with improbable events but failed on most of the passive sentences. The 5-year-olds based their interpretation on the language sentence content but also had some problems with the passive sentences describing improbable events.

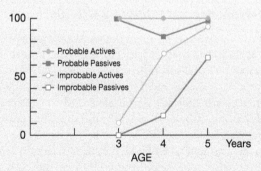

out *The cat was bitten by the duck*, which was the expected action based on their knowledge about cats and ducks. With another group of children, the researcher said *naughty duck* or *poor cat* before the sentence was presented, and these children let the duck bite the cat (MacWhinney, 1982). Whether they noticed the word order at all is uncertain – children are usually closer to school age by the time they understand passive sentences.

Early Sentence Construction

The age when children start to use sentences varies widely. Some children use many utterances with two or more words before the age of 16 months; others have few or no such utterances even past the age of 2 years (Bates et al., 1995). In addition, the transition from single to multiword utterances can take quite a long time. Ramer (1976) found that the time between the child's first two-word utterances until 20 percent of the utterances consisted of two or more words ranged from 1½ to 9 months. Since all the children developed normal speech, the variation in time did not reflect any permanent difference in language skills.

In moving to multi-word utterances, children use thematically related **successive single-word utterances**. In the following example Allison is 18 months old and her father had used a knife to cut up a piece of peach lying in the bowl of a spoon (Bloom, 1973). Allison hands him a new peach and a spoon, and says:

> *Daddy.*
> *Peach.*
> *Cut.*

This type of successive single-word utterance differs from children's later multi-word utterances in that the words are not connected by an intonation contour. Little by little, the pace of children's word production increases, inter-word pauses get progressively shorter and several words fall within the same intonation contour (Peters, 1995; Scollon, 1976).

According to Tomasello (1992, 2003), verbs have a core function in children's grammatical constructions as structural elements that express *intent*. Because a verb implies that someone performs an action and someone or something else may receive it, verbs represent an early conceptual framework for constructing sentences. The verb *to kick* entails that someone does the kicking and something or someone else is being kicked, such as a boy kicking a ball. The verb *to give* implies that someone gives, that something is given and that someone else is the recipient of what is being given, for example a girl who gives an apple to her teacher. With verbs as a basis, children learn to use constructions such as "X kicks Y," "X gives Y," "X pushes Y," and so forth, linking verbs to words that indicate specific people, places, objects, points in time, and so on. Once children's utterances include a greater number of words, more elements become explicit as well, for example, *The boy kicks the ball through the window,* or *The girl gives a red apple to the math teacher.*

Children's language is creative but young children have a small language repertoire. One study involving four 2-year-olds found that 20–40 percent of their utterances were word sequences that they had used before, and 40–50 percent of their utterances were identical to a previous utterance except for one single point of variation (Lieven et al., 2009). This means that they use strategies that worked for them in the past when solving communicative challenges. They also use utterances they themselves have frequently used or heard others use for a particular purpose as *formulas* or models for constructing new sentences (Bannard and Lieven, 2012). The sentence *Can I have apple?*, for example, can provide the formula "Can I have X?", where X can be apple, juice, book, ball, and so on. Other typical early formulas are "Where is X?" and "Shall we X?" (Tomasello, 2006).

Formulas are useful during very early development, but if children were to base their language exclusively on formulas, their language would become fairly stereotyped – as in the case of many children with autism spectrum disorder (Boucher, 2012). Children notice that other people use different types of sentence constructions and assume that there is a reason for doing so, analogous to the *principle of contrast* in word learning. The child wants to find out why the other person chooses a particular sentence construction, that is, the intent behind using structure A rather than structure B (Tomasello, 2006). Formulas thus make it possible to exploit previously established sentence structures, while the principle of contrast encourages the use of new grammatical constructions.

Young children thus construct their own sentences from observing the language of others. They take notice of single words and larger parts of sentences, and use them actively, even if they fail to understand the entire sentence. Some of the sentences children use consist of adults' expansions of their own utterances (see below), but they produce many sentences they have never heard before. Children constantly create more or less new meaningful structures based on the context of the conversation and their own goals and objectives in what they express.

More Complex Sentences

At the age of 2, most children have started to use simple sentences, and the length and complexity of their utterances gradually increases toward school age. Their initial sentence-building strategies continue to develop and expand, and their own productivity becomes increasingly important. Complex utterances begin to emerge as combinations of simpler sentences. Sentences that previously were uttered separately turn into a single sentence. *Daddy car* and *Daddy drive* becomes *Daddy drive car*, so that the common element *Daddy* is only used once. Tomasello's daughter Travis combined the formulas *Look at X* and *Pete eat X* into the sentence *Look at Pete eating a bone* (Tomasello, 1992). The children's language becomes more efficient because they can include more information in a single utterance.

Children produce increasingly more intricate sentences, such as *I saw the neighbor's horse jump over the fence, which is broken*. An increase in complexity is particularly pronounced between the ages of 5 and 7, but complexity continues to increase throughout school age (Berman, 2007; Nippold, 1998). The context also influences sentence structure: young adolescents used much longer and more complex sentences when they retold fables than when they engaged in conversations about topics like family, friends, hobbies, sports and travel (Nippold et al., 2014).

Word Classes and Inflections

Word inflections mark important information about the word – for example tense or plurality – and its role in the utterance. To master the language, children have to learn the inflections of their language. Children learning English and many other languages have to learn that verbs can either be conjugated regularly (e.g., *play – played – have played*) or *irregularly* (e.g., *go – went – have gone*). Children learning Chinese or other East Asian languages have to learn the functions of classifier inflections. To ask for one apple, they have to say *yi ge pinguo* ('one unit apple'). Without the classifier *ge* (which would be ungrammatical), it is not clear if the child means one apple, a piece of apple or a bag of apples (Allan, 1977; Li et al., 2010).

The words in children's earliest utterances are without inflections. It is only once children are well underway to using sentences that they begin to inflect words and include function words such as *over* and *under*. During early language development, children use both regular and irregular verbs, but only in their simple form. They appear to perceive conjugations of the same verb as different words, such as *do* and *did*. Around the age of 2–3, children begin to *overregulate* the conjugation of verbs (Marcus, 1995). They may say *goed* instead of *went*, even if they previously said *went*. It seems that children first begin to learn the general rules of verb conjugation at around this age, and that they still have not understood that there are exceptions. Other word classes are treated similarly, for example *two mouses*. This also has to do with the fact that children are used to making mistakes and adjust what they say during early language development. Their "errors" are the result of new insights, and they need time to identify the boundaries of these new regularities they have discovered.

Some of the systematic aspects of language take a long time to learn. Related words belonging to different word classes, for example, usually share the same stem, such as in *saw* and *sawing*, making it possible to *derive* a word class based on the stem of a word from a different word class. Derwing and Baker (1986) found that 25 of 40 English-speaking children between the age of 6 and 8 had learned to add *-er* to the end of a verb in order to indicate an individual performing an action, such as *to run* and *a runner*. Twenty-two of 40 11-year-olds were able to derive adjectives from nouns by adding *-y*, such as *greed* and *greedy*, while 32 of 40 adolescents aged 12–17 managed to derive adverbs by attaching the suffix *-ly*, as in *serious* and *seriously*. Younger children are only able to derive words from well-familiar verbs, while older children are also able to do so with recently learned verbs (Lieven et al., 2003).

Different Views on Children's Sentence Construction

The transition from single words to sentences and the acquisition of syntax and grammar is the most discussed topic in language development. The main division runs between nativism, which claims that children acquire abstract grammatical rules by way of an innate *universal grammar*, and usage-based theory and emergentism, which maintain that children *construct* language based on their cognitive resources and experience with language. Nativism and usage-based theory thus have very different views on how children come to master grammar. *Overregulation* (see above) has been given special attention because children produce word inflections they have not heard from adults. Nativists argue that the overregulation reflects the development of a linguistic rule system based on universal gram mar. Children forget the exceptions and use the rules on them as well (Pinker, 1994). According to the usage-based theory, children initially learn to inflect one item at a time, rather than starting with a general rule, and use *analogy* when they inflect new words. Overregulation occurs because children have not yet learned the different conjugations of verbs and overregulate by choosing the most common ones. Thus, usage-based theory views overregulation as a result of the learning process itself. Both nativism and usage-based theory are able to explain children's overregulation and the presence of overregulation can therefore not be used to distinguish between the theories (Ambridge and Lieven, 2011).

On the other hand, according to the theory of a universal grammar, a child who has learned to use a particular grammatical structure should be able to use it in any linguistic context – the content is irrelevant (Radford, 1990). One study, however, found the mastery of passive sentence structure was not the same across verbs: 80 percent of a group of 5-year-olds understood passive sentences with *to hit*, while only 30 percent understood sentences with *to follow*. This supports a usage-based theory (Tomasello, 2003).

7

Language in Use

The functions of language are rooted in the intention to communicate something to someone else. The object may be to give or to obtain information, to get someone to do something, to maintain the conversation, and so on. Toddlers talk mostly to adults, and their conversations often revolve around the child's activities together with the adult. Their language use typically involves getting someone else to do something (*take*), expressing agreement or disagreement with someone else's suggestion (*yes*, *no*), expressing what something is (*that car*), and what they intend to do (*I throw*). They also respond to their parents' *yes/no* questions (Snow et al., 1996). About a third of all toddlers' utterances consist of descriptions and statements, compared with 80–90 percent among adults (Dore, 1977; Miller, 1981).

Children also use language as a tool to explore the environment and regulate their own behavior by commenting on objects and their own actions without any apparent communicative intent (see Book 4, *Cognition, Intelligence and Learning*, Chapter 19). Vygotsky (1962) considers this a step toward children's **internalization** of language and other people's regulation of their behavior. In one study, 21 percent of the utterances of 4-year-olds in dialogue with each other had elements of **self-regulation**, including the use of "monologues" to guide themselves through play activities such as building a house. However, it varied considerably: some of the 4-year-olds used a lot of self-regulating speech, others almost none (Schober-Peterson and Johnson, 1991).

Conversation Skills

Conversation requires many skills. Conversation partners must have a common focus, agree on a topic, understand what the other person can

DOI: 10.4324/9781003292524-7

understand and communicate, and provide a relevant response to the other person's input. Conversation skills include strategies to express communicative intent and regulate the conversation, such as taking initiative, answering, turntaking, clearing up misunderstandings and ending the conversation. In early dialogues, the adult assumes practically all responsibility for keeping the conversation going, such as in the following dialogue between Sean and his mother (Dore, 1986):

M: *Okay, let's go play bally?* (Both go toward family room) *Wanna play bouncy ball?*
S: *Ba(ll).* /b_/
M: *Okay. You get the ball there.* (Points to ball)
S: (Hands the ball to her)
M: *Sit down. Here. Like this.* (Positions Sean in front of her and spreads out legs in V-shape) *Here we go.* (Rolls ball to Sean)
S: (Clutches the ball) *Ba(ll).* /b_/ (Pushes ball toward his mother)
M: *Nice. Good boy, Sean. That a boy.* (Rolls ball back to him).

During early conversations, the adult is in control while at the same time supporting the child's participation. Once children's vocabulary increases, adults ask many questions they usually know the answer to. This helps children take turns and produce a relevant utterance, even if they do not remember the entire context. Even 18-month-olds seem to understand that the rising intonation of a question means that it is their turn. Generally, toddlers respond far more often to questions than to purely narrative statements by the adult. Twenty-month-olds respond to about one-third of their parents' questions, whereas 29–36-month-olds respond almost twice as often (Pan and Snow, 1999).

Conversations between toddlers usually do not last long, at least not about the same topic. They have difficulty taking turns without getting support, and understanding how the utterances in a conversation relate to each other – many utterances of younger preschool children are unsuccessful attempts at dialogue (Nelson and Gruendel, 1979; Schober-Peterson and Johnson, 1991). Successful conversations are often closely linked to children's actions, such as the following dialogue between two 3-year-olds, Alex and Nicki (Karmiloff and Karmiloff-Smith, 2001, p. 154):

A: *I'm gonna put it there.*
N: *Over there.*

A: *On the green box.*
N: *Yeah, put it on top.*
A: *You wanna do it?*
N: *Okay.*

With age, children contribute more equally to the conversation. They take more initiative in the dialogue and adults do not need to adapt as much to the child's level of comprehension. Dialogues increase in length and there are fewer breaks in communication. The increase in communicative equality seems to be related to the fact that adults leave children with more of the responsibility for keeping the dialogue alive. Whether this is the reason for children's increased contributions or the result of their improved skills is impossible to say – children and adults probably influence another.

Older children, too, can have difficulty maintaining focus on a single topic over time. In a study of 7–12-year-olds, the children were to pretend to be hosts in a television program. The adults who were interviewed by the children were instructed to answer their questions but not to respond to any more than what the children asked about. The children who did best asked many open questions. Several children were unable to keep the conversation going for the designated

Children spend much of their time in conversations with parents.

Figure 7.1 Experiment on referential communication.

The illustration shows a typical experimental situation examining children's ability to describe photographs, geometric shapes and patterns, maps and the like, so someone else who cannot see the referent is able to find or recreate it.

4 minutes, and some of the adults failed to refrain from helping by asking questions of their own, although they had been told not to do so (Schley and Snow, 1992). This shows how slowly these skills evolve and how natural it is for adults to help children in their language development.

Successful conversations require that the communication partners take the other's perspective and adapt the language they produce to the language skills and knowledge of the other person. This adaptive process begins early on. Four-year-olds talk differently to 2-year-olds than to peers and adults (Shatz and Gelman, 1973). In studies of **"referential communication,"** one of the conversation partners has to describe something in such a way that the other person, without having seen it, can find it among several similar objects (Figure 7.1). Adults generally have no difficulty describing geometric shapes so another adult can identify them. The descriptions of preschool children, however, tend to be private and ambiguous, and even adults do not always succeed in finding the correct shape based on their descriptions (Glucksberg et al., 1966). With age, children's descriptions become more precise, and they improve at conveying referential information.

Clarification and Repair

Conversations typically involve smaller and larger misunderstandings, which must be detected and resolved to avoid breakdowns in communication, and negotiation is part of the meaning making. Parents ask their children to clarify things even before starting to talk with them about matters beyond the immediate situation (Pan and Snow, 1999). Starting at a relatively early age, children, too, begin to "repair" or change statements they have discovered to be wrong or that are misunderstood by the person they are talking to. In a study of 2–3 year-olds, Clark (1992) registered between 30 and 50 repairs of this type for each child within a half-hour observation:

Kate (2;8): *What – who's that?*
Zoe (2;11): *Not the – I don't mean the new one. The old one.*

Another study found that a third of all the clarifying questions parents asked children aged 2;6 were not "genuine" questions in the sense that the parents did not wait for an answer. Because the children's statements had been unclear, their parents asked them to explain what they meant but failed to wait for an answer, probably because they did not think the child would be able to do so (Shatz and O'Reilly, 1990). The parents tried to guess what the children intended to say, rather than making excessive demands on them. A third of the children's answers did not clarify the misunderstanding and many questions were simply met affirmatively. In some cases, the children asked their parents for clarification and usually received a reply. Nevertheless, this rarely clarified the misunderstanding because the children did not wait for the parents' answer.

Misunderstandings often arise in conversation with preschool children because they do not take sufficient account of the other person's knowledge. Until the age of 5, children rarely notice that the other person seems confused or puzzled at something they have said, and they rarely express that there is something they have not understood. Even 9-year-olds have difficulty discovering ambiguities in what is being said (Lloyd et al., 1995).

Conversations and Activities

Changes in children's conversation skills are reflected in the activities they take part in. The first conversations occur in simple activities that place few demands on children's participation. During **preschool**

age, children increasingly participate in smaller and larger groups in connection with games and other activities. Spending time together with peers places new demands on children's ability to maintain conversations without the help usually provided by adults. Children's increased competence leads to greater linguistic freedom and opportunities to use their imagination and initiate play activities, but also more responsibility to adapt their communication to the others and to the situation. Once they start in school, children become part of a broader social reality and have to cope with many new situations and communicative codes. They must learn how to speak in class, in the street together with their peers and with grandma when she comes to visit. During adolescence, with its youth culture and emotions, conversations with peers become a main activity. Thus, the acquisition of conversation skills is closely linked to **enculturation** in general, as well as to children's and adolescents' developing understanding of themselves and others in a social and cultural context.

Narratives

Story-telling is a common human activity and part of everyday life. Many child–parent conversations are about something that has happened, about what the child or other people did and experienced, and these are important for the child's understanding of the world (Bruner, 1991). A narrative is a story, a representation of a chain of events in time and space in which people (or other characters) engage in action and have intentions, motives, interests and emotions (Labov, 1972). The development of narrative abilities is related to **autobiographical memory** (see Book 4, *Cognition, Intelligence and Learning*, Chapter 10) and the development of the self (see Book 7, *Social Relations, Self-awareness and Identity*, Part III).

Children begin to share experiences early on, both to tell what is happening and to get help understanding events, starting with declarative pointing (see Chapter 5) and followed by the early language dialogues. Prior to the narrative below, Philip (aged 10) had let his budgerigar out of its cage. It landed on 18-month-old David's head, and this had frightened him. The boys' mother encouraged David to tell the story to his father, Herb (Clark, 2016, p. 321):

M: *Did you see Philip's bird? Can you tell Herb?*
D: *Head, head, head.*

M: *What landed on your head?*
D: *Bird.*

David began with the story's emotional climax – something happened to his head. His mother helped him bring in another character (the bird) and thus created a slightly larger context. Beginning with the emotional highpoint is typical for children's early narratives, also fragments and lack of coherence. The "fairy tale structure" of narratives, beginning with "once upon a time" and ending with "they lived happily ever after," only develops much later.

At around 3 years of age, children begin to tell more coherent stories, but younger children's stories tend to be descriptive and characters are mainly represented by their physical and external attributes, and many of their narratives lack a temporal structure (Küntay, 2004). Questions from the adult may support coherence in the child's narrative (Silva et al., 2014). Mothers of 3-year-olds asked for more information and repeated the child's utterance more often than mothers of 5-year-olds when co-constructing narratives, as the older children needed less help (Zevenbergen et al., 2016). Five-year-olds include more information about the characters' mental state – their thoughts, feelings and motives – but references to thoughts and perceptions are rare even among 5–6-year-olds (Nelson, 2009; Nicolopoulou and Richner, 2007).

Through school age, children's narratives are gradually longer and more elaborated (see examples in Box 7.1). The children are also becoming more independent in their narrative construction. A mother and a child of school age may have quite different narratives of the same event, but the child may still need help to include emotional and evaluative aspects (Fivush et al., 2008; Veneziano, 2016). Toward adolescence, narratives become more cohesive, detailed and evaluative (Habermas and de Silveira, 2008; Ukrainetz et al., 2005). Narrative skills are important in adolescence because schools expect students to be able to read and retell what they have read. In addition, adolescents spend increasing amounts of time in **self-disclosure** (see Book 7, *Social Relations, Self-awareness and Identity*, Chapter 21) and telling stories about themselves and others in an effort to achieve acknowledgement and emotional support (Nippold et al., 2014).

Box 7.1   Fictitious Stories by School-Aged Children (Ukrainetz et al., 2005)

A total of 293 children aged 5–12 years were asked to tell a story from the same five pictures from *Test of Narrative Language* (Gillam and Pearson, 2004):

1   A boy is sitting in bed looking at a clock with a distressed expression.
2   The boy is spilling milk as he looks at a wall clock.
3   The boy is snapping a shoelace while putting on shoes.
4   The boy is running after the departing school bus.
5   The boy is walking up the school steps and a woman in a suit is standing outside looking at her watch sternly.

The stories below are typical of each age group.

5–6 Years

Once there was a little boy. He was sleeping in his bed. And he went to go eat his breakfast and accidentally took the string out of his shoe and accidentally broke. And then he tried to go to school with the bus. But the bus leaved already. And he had to walk to school. And then the teacher said he was late.

7–9 Years

One morning Bob woke up. And it was twenty after seven. And he was running late for school. And he started pouring a bowl of cereal. And he wasn't paying attention. And he spilled some milk. So he started to clean it up. And then he said I just can't have breakfast this morning. And he went and got dressed. He accidentally tore his shoelace. So he got some tape and taped it. When he got his backpack and ran to the school bus stop he missed the school bus. So he had to run all the way to school. Her teacher got mad at him because he was late. She was wondering if he would come. The end.

10–12 Years

One morning a kid woke up. And his name was Todd. He got up and looked at his clock and it turned out he was almost late for school And so he got out of bed. And got dressed hurriedly. And he went into the kitchen. This is where he poured his favorite cereal was out. So he had to do his least favorite which is crunchymunchys. And while he was looking at the clock worrying about time he poured milk over all his cereal. After he got dressed, he started to tie his shoe. And the shoelace snapped. After a long of trying to repair the shoelace he decided to give up. He put on his backpack ran outside and discovered his school bus had raced ahead of him. After a long and treacherous time of walking to school the teacher said he was late. And he had to spend the recess inside.

Narrative skills are not always included but may be a useful element in the **assessment** of language abilities (Norbury and Bishop, 2003). Children from language minorities may have lower narrative skills than their peers and intervention in preschool may give them a better start in school (Petersen and Spencer, 2016). Children and adolescents with disabilities involving communication and language also tend to struggle with narrative construction, including those with intellectual disability (van Bysterveldt et al., 2012), speech and language disorders (Paul et al., 1996; Soto and Hartmann, 2006) and autism spectrum disorders (Baixauli et al., 2016). A low narrative competence may lead to poorer understanding of personal and other social events, and enculturation in general. It may also make it more difficult for children and adolescents with disabilities to tell about personal events and use narration to cope with difficult situations. Studies show that intervention with story retelling in preschool and school may improve narrative abilities (Petersen, 2011; Petersen et al., 2014).

8

Child-directed Language

Adults are children's main source of knowledge about language, and parents vary with regard to how much they speak and in their adaptation when they speak to infants and toddlers. Early **child-directed speech** is characterized by many short utterances, simple sentence structures and few grammatical errors. Vowels are extended in length. The pronunciation is clear, with distinctly marked stresses on important words, exaggerated intonation and a somewhat lighter vocal register than in speech directed at adults (Fernald and Mazzie, 1991). The intonation seems to draw infants' attention to the speech (Spinelli et al., 2017). Deaf mothers slow down signing in interactions with their infants and toddlers and use rhythmic, slightly exaggerated movements and more repetitions than when they communicate with adults (Masataka, 1992).

Repetition is common when adults talk to young children, but they rarely repeat the same thing in the same way. Parents change their utterances a little or repeat parts of them, producing **variation sets** with slightly different information, such as this mother who speaks to her 14-month-old child (Brodsky et al., 2007, p. 834):

> M: *You got to push them to school.*
> *Push them.*
> *Push them to school.*
> *Take them to school.*
> *You got to take them to school.*

Parental self-repetition without variation does not provide new information unless the utterance was not heard (or seen) by the child the first time, but partial repetitions may function to highlight

DOI: 10.4324/9781003292524-8

prominent sentence elements. A study of 12 mothers' speech to their 2-year-olds found that much of their speech included a small number of "frames" with the same first or last word like *In X, What do X, Are you X, It's X, Let's X, Look X, I think X* or *If X*, as well as many fragments and reduced sentences, consistent with use of variation sets (Cameron-Faulkner et al., 2003).

Repetition of what children say is often combined with recast and **expansion**. For example, if the child says *Daddy cup*, the adult may reformulate and expand it to *Yes, that's Daddy's cup standing on the table*. In this way, the adult shows the child how the utterance has been interpreted, while at the same time giving it a more complete grammatical form. Expansion links new words to the ones the child has already learned; recasting may function as negative evidence and correction (Chouinard and Clark, 2003; Nelson et al., 1973). Both have been shown to be effective strategies in intervention for children with language impairment (Cleave et al., 2015; Nelson, 2001). In sum, this underlines the fact that children do not simply mimic the sentences they have heard before but construct language based on information from different sources (von Tetzchner et al., 2008).

How much parents talk with their children varies considerably. In one study, the number of utterances to 1- to 3-year-olds varied between 34 and 793 utterances per hour. Assuming that children at this age are awake 14 hours a day, some children will hear 476 utterances per day, others 11,102. In the course of 1 year, this adds up to anywhere between 175,000 and 4 million utterances (Hart and Risley, 1992). In a study of families with low **socioeconomic** background, caregiver speech directed at their 19-month-old-child varied from 670 to 12,000 words per day, and the total speech accessible to the child from 2,000 to 29,000 words. The amount of child-directed speech seemed to matter: there was a positive **correlation** between child-directed speech at 19 months and vocabulary size based on a parent-completed schedule at 24 months (Weisleder and Fernald, 2013). Children of talkative mothers tend to talk a lot themselves and follow up their mother's topic more often than children with less talkative mothers (Hoff, 2006). However, individual differences do not only reflect parents' talkativeness, but also the children's language skills and their reactions to being talked to.

The adaptations of child-directed speech are particularly prominent in the first phase of speech development and they are gradually reduced as the child's language skills improve. By the time children reach the age of 5 years, adults no longer adapt the stress and intonation of their speech when speaking to children. The results cited above indicate that the amount of parents' speech to children matters, and exaggerated stress and intonation seem to help guide infants' attention to the speech. Parents' use of vocabulary affects the words children learn (Rowe, 2012; see Chapter 6). However, it is still debated how crucial the special characteristics of child-directed speech are for children's language development. Studies have found that the features typical of Western child-directed speech are not as prominent among adult speakers in other language communities, suggesting that this type of speech may be useful but not essential to children's language development (Schaffer, 1989). Children's own spontaneous language use in conversations may be more important. Hoff-Ginsberg (1990) found that the development of children's syntax was best supported by parents who engaged them in linguistic interaction. The structure of the parents' language was less important. This suggests that parents are not so much direct models, but rather supportive interlocutors in social and meaningful contexts.

9

Gender Differences

Many studies show that girls on average develop comprehension and use of language earlier than boys (e.g., Kimura, 1999; Zambrana et al., 2012), and language disorders are more prevalent among boys than girls (see Book 1, *Theoretical Perspectives and Methodology*, Chapter 32 p. 60). Differences are observable from the start. There is no difference in the onset of gesture use but girls start to use word-gesture combinations and spoken sentences about 3 months earlier than boys (Özçalışˌkan and Goldin-Meadow, 2010). Differences in language skills in favor of girls tend to become more evident in school age. Some features that differ between adult males and females first become pronounced after the age of 10, but certain aspects of language use can be observed as early as preschool age (Ladegaard and Bleses, 2003). Six-year-old girls, for example, make more informative statements and talk more about emotions than boys, while boys make more statements involving control (Tenenbaum et al., 2011).

Researchers have unsuccessfully attempted to find a neurological basis for **gender differences** in language development (see Book 2, *Genes, Foetal Development and Early Neurological Development*, Chapter 17). **Sex** hormones seem to influence language development but the mechanism behind this is unknown (Schaadt et al., 2015). The slightly earlier development of girls' language skills may also be related to the fact that they participate more in language-related activities, while boys more often take part in physical play (see Book 7, *Social Relations, Self-awareness and Identity*, Chapter 27). Studies have also shown that, starting at an early age, parents speak somewhat differently to boys than to girls, for example they interrupt girls more often than boys when they talk. Fathers are more directive when they speak to their sons and use more loving expressions such as *my little pet* when

DOI: 10.4324/9781003292524-9

talking to their daughters (Andersen, 1990; Gleason and Greif, 1983). Additionally, there are differences in how mothers tell stories and talk about feelings with boys and with girls. It is likely that these influences contribute to **shaping** some gender-specific language use (Leaper and Smith, 2004).

10

Multilingualism

More than half of all children grow up as multilingual (Grosjean, 2010). **Multilingualism** is defined as the mastery of two or more languages at the level of a native speaker. In its most common form, it involves two languages. In *bilingual first language acquisition* the child is exposed to two languages from birth; in *early second language acquisition*, exposition to the second language begins between the age of 1;6 and 4 years (De Houwer, 2009). When bilingualism is practiced *within* the family, one or both of the two languages are usually part of the external language environment. When bilingualism is practiced *between* the family and the society, the family speaks a different language than most of the community around them. In such cases of **minority language** use, the family often has contact with others who speak the same language, although some children grow up with a home language that is spoken by only a few people in their environment. Moving from one country to another can involve language loss because the use of the first language becomes limited (Bialystok, 2001; De Houwer, 2009). Internationally adopted toddlers may experience a total shift of language, as expressed by one parent: "She didn't have a word of English; we didn't have a word of Vietnamese" (McAndrew and Malley-Keighran, 2017, p. 89). It can be difficult to distinguish language disorders from the language problems of minority language children who have little experience with many topics in the majority language and have received inadequate education (Paradis, 2010; Scheidnes and Tuller, 2016).

Children growing up with two languages must learn two phonological systems, vocabularies and grammars, and when to use each of the two. Children who learn a spoken language and a sign language must learn a system of sounds and a system of movements

DOI: 10.4324/9781003292524-10

(Petitto et al., 2001). This is generally no more difficult than learning the sounds or movements of a single language. Children who learn both languages from the start will master both phonological systems equally well if their exposure is the same. Children with both a home language and an outside language are usually exposed to the home language first. They may struggle a bit initially but by the age of 5 children have usually mastered both phonological systems (Werker and Byers-Heinlein, 2008).

Bilingual children acquire their first words at about the same age as monolingual children, but they need to build a far greater inventory of word forms if they are to master each language as well as monolinguals. Their vocabulary develops a bit more slowly in each of the two languages compared with monolingual children, partly because they do not learn the corresponding words simultaneously but in separate language situations. They also have less time and experience with each language compared with those who learn a single language only. Looking at the two languages in context, however, the picture changes. Many words are initially learned in one language only, but even if words familiar in both languages are only counted once, the total vocabulary of bilingual children often exceeds that of their monolingual peers (Bialystok and Luk, 2012; Hoff et al., 2012).

Bilingual children also need to learn which words correspond to each other in the two languages. Saunders (1988) suggests that up to the age of 2, bilingual children have one common set of words among the two languages, but studies have shown that as early as their second year, many bilingual children use words with the same meaning in both languages, for example *bola* (Portuguese) and *ball* (English), or *Brot* (German) and *pain* (French). Sometimes they say both words, such as *heiss hot*. Until the age of 2, the percentage of words common to both languages is relatively small – typically 20 to 30 percent – but from this age on, it increases significantly (De Houwer, 2009). Grosjean (1982) tells of a 2-year-old girl who combined *chaud* and *hot* into *shot*, although this type of language mixing, also called code-mixing, is rare. Problems with codemixing usually have to do with words that have the same form but different meanings, such as *gift* in English and *Gift* (poison) in German.

Sometimes bilingual children construct sentences with words from both languages, such as *Und ich bin boy*, but there are major individual differences. Some children never mix languages, others do it half of the time. When children mix languages, their parents usually mix the two languages as well and sometimes even encourage it, leaving the division between the two languages somewhat indistinct (De Houwer, 2009; Lanza, 1997). Bilingual toddlers generally use the correct language when talking to another person 80–90 percent of the time (De Houwer, 2009).

Languages have different syntax and the order of acquisition of grammatical structures essentially corresponds to the monolingual development in each language. The phase without word inflections (see Chapter 6) seems to be shorter for bilingual than for monolingual children, perhaps because they become aware of the variation in word forms at an earlier point (Genese and Nicoladis, 2007). Since languages differ in their development, bilingual children can to some degree express different grammatical relationships in the two languages. For example, Slobin (1973) reports about two girls who used locative expressions far earlier in Hungarian than in Serbo-Croatian, which has an extremely complex system of locative prepositions. Bilingual children sometimes transfer the word order of the dominant language to the other language for a period.

It has been argued that bilingualism causes problems if the native language has not been acquired before the next language is learned (Hansegård, 1968), but studies show that bilingualism has a positive rather than a negative impact on cognitive development (Bialystok et al., 2012). Bilingual children must learn the different ways their languages categorize the world and realize early on that there is more than one perspective to the same thing. This may be the reason that bilingual children tend to develop better than average **executive functions** and a flexibility in solving problems and thinking creatively. They consistently do better on tasks that require selective attention and inhibition of responses (Bialystok, 2001).

Bilingualism can be harmonic and successful – there are many examples of children who benefit from growing up with two languages in an active bilingual environment. However, bilingualism does not come entirely by itself; the child must get adequate exposure to both languages. When bilingualism occurs within the family, conversation with both parents becomes more critical for children's language development than in the case of monolingual families. De Houwer (2009) writes about an English-speaking father who spoke little with his daughter because he travelled much. The mother spoke Flemish with the daughter. The father argued on the basis of the theory of an innate universal grammar (see Chapter 6) that the extent of language stimulation did not matter and that the daughter would develop his language anyway. The result was that at 3 years she neither understood nor used English.

In many countries professionals advise parents to use only a single language with their child, often a language other than that spoken by the parents among themselves. Sometimes, one or both parents are not particularly good at expressing themselves in this language. Using the majority language may lead to a poorer and less varied language environment than if the child grew up with parents speaking their native language, cause the child to feel rejected by being excluded from the parents' language, give rise to more emotional distance and impede the child's relationship with the parents. It is far better to ensure a solid language environment in both languages within and outside the family (De Houwer, 2009).

Bilingualism is as common among children with disabilities as among nondisabled children but research is limited (Kay-Raining Bird et al., 2016). The professional advice of using one language with the child is often given to parents of children with disabilities, as expressed by this Chinese mother of a 3-year-old with autism spectrum disorder (Yu, 2016a, p. 428):

> *And that speech therapist would say, uh, the way we talk, in two languages, affects his language development. She kept insisting to us that it wasn't the problem of having or not having one–one–one therapy but that we need to speak English at home.*

The advice is based on the belief that it is easier for children with language impairment to learn only one language, that the child may be confused and that the home language will interfere with learning the majority language – beliefs that are not supported by research (Peña, 2016; Yu, 2013, 2016b). Bilingual development does not safeguard against disorders but neither does it involve any increased **vulnerability** (De Houwer, 2013; Kohnert, 2010). Children with **Down syndrome**, for example, have no more problems with bilingualism than other children (Kay Raining-Bird et al., 2005; Ostad, 2008). Autism spectrum disorder implies difficulties with communication and language but children with this disorder are not negatively affected by a bilingual situation (Lund et al., 2017). However, the exposure to the two languages matters. One study found that children with simultaneous bilingualism do as well in both languages as monolingual children with language impairment in their language, while children with sequential bilingualism do less well in the second language. This is usually the majority language of the society but depends on exposure to each of the languages, and they may need more exposure to the weaker language (Kay-Raining Bird et al., 2016). Language intervention has positive effects but interventions in one language show little generalization to the other, so bilingual children with language impairment often need intervention in both languages (Ebert et al., 2014). In addition, including the home language may increase the parental language input and the family's engagement in the child's bilingual development (Verdon et al., 2016). Today, professionals still tend to regard it as difficult to support bilingual development in children with communication and language impairment but in many countries there seems to be a trend toward more bilingual special education (Marinova-Todd et al., 2016).

11

Language in Other Modalities

Language and speech are not the same. Language is independent of a particular **sensory modality** and can be acquired in various forms. Some children need a visual form of communication due to hearing impairment (Mellon et al., 2015), while others have motor impairments or other physical disabilities and need **augmentative and alternative communication** (von Tetzchner and Martinsen, 2000).

Sign Language

Many deaf children need sign language (for a discussion of different language forms, see Book 3, *Perceptual and Motor Development*, Chapter 4). The developmental process is similar in sign and speech, and like spoken language, sign language development depends on the language environment. Deaf parents who sign adapt their child-directed signing similar to hearing parents' child-directed speech (see Chapter 8). However, 90 percent of deaf children's parents are hearing and to support their child's signing they first need to learn the national sign language (Napier et al., 2007). They therefore have less developed sign language skills and also adapt their child-directed signing to a lesser degree than deaf parents (Masataka, 1992; Spencer and Harris, 2006). One study found that deaf children of deaf parents showed a typical gradual course of language development, while the increased exposure to sign language when they entered a school for deaf children led to accelerated sign language development in deaf children with hearing parents. The older they were when they entered the school, the lower they later scored on a test of sign language grammar (Novogrodsky et al., 2017).

DOI: 10.4324/9781003292524-11

Provided they have a good signing environment, deaf children who develop sign language begin to use the first signs and multi-sign utterances at about the same age as hearing children speak their first words and phrases (Petitto and Marentette, 1991). They acquire a sign repertoire that matches the vocabulary of hearing children, but with a somewhat larger proportion of verbs, maybe because the manual form of sign languages makes action and motion more salient (Hoiting, 2006; Rinaldi et al., 2014). Without a sign language environment, sign development will be limited (Coppola, 2002; Kegl and Iwata, 1989). Studies show that deaf parents use a richer sign vocabulary and that deaf children with deaf parents have a more developed vocabulary and use more different handshapes than deaf children with hearing parents (Lu et al., 2016). The grammars of signed and spoken language differ considerably within the same society. This means that the development paths differ somewhat, but as long as deaf children grow up in a sign language environment, the complexity of their signed utterances will increase in line with the spoken utterances of their peers. Thus, the development of speech and signing is comparable in these areas as well.

Manual Signs and Graphic Symbols for Children with Severe Speech and Language Impairment

Also some groups of children with normal hearing may need another communication form than speech (Smith and Murray, 2016; von Tetzchner, 2018; von Tetzchner and Martinsen, 2000). Severe motor impairments may prevent children from speaking or make their speech unintelligible. They must rely on graphic symbols, written words and letters that can support and supplement or replace speech. The cognitive abilities of children in this group vary considerably; some motor disabled children with little or no speech have cognitive abilities in the normal range and can follow the regular school curriculum, others have intellectual disability (Stadskleiv et al., 2017). They may also need other forms of intervention but the function of augmentative and alternative communication (AAC) is to give children with disabilities opportunities for language development, although in an atypical manner (von Tetzchner and Grove, 2003).

Children with autism spectrum disorder, intellectual disability or severe language impairment may also have difficulty acquiring speech

Early sign language promotes communication and language development in children with Down syndrome.

normally, even if they grow up in an adequate language environment and receive speech therapy. Many of them benefit from learning manual signs or graphic symbols (von Tetzchner and Martinsen, 2000). Although they do not develop signed or aided language skills comparable to typically developing children, they can improve their communication skills significantly, and often their spoken language as well, provided they have an adequately adapted language environment (von Tetzchner and Stadskleiv, 2016). In many countries, most children with Down syndrome, for example, receive early intervention with manual signs (Clibbens, 2001; Launonen, 1996; Wright et al., 2013).

Augmentative and Alternative Communication and Speech Development

There is a long-standing controversy whether the acquisition of manual signs or graphic symbols can inhibit speech development but all the evidence shows that language use promotes language development, independent of the modality being used. In fact, some parents teach their normally developing, hearing toddlers "baby signs" to boost their cognitive and linguistic development (Acredolo and Goodwyn, 2009; Pizer et al., 2007). Studies of deaf children show that sign language promotes both the development of speech and literacy (Miller, 2010; Strong and Prinz, 1997). Similarly, studies of children with severe language and communication impairments show that intervention with manual signs and graphic symbols promotes rather than inhibits the development of speech (Clibbens, 2001; Drager et al., 2010; Millar et al., 2006; Schlosser and Wendt, 2008).

12

Language Disorders

Most children develop language without any particular problems, but some struggle on their way into language (see Book 1, *Theoretical Perspectives and Methodology*, Chapter 32). There are children who have such severe problems that they affect the children's social functioning and learning as well as their emotional functioning and **self-image**. Disorders involving impairment of comprehension in particular affect the acquisition of knowledge and social skills (Law et al., 2007). Articulation disorders alone can also affect children's learning and development, partly because the children may be perceived as younger than they are or to have lower cognitive functioning than they actually do. Children with language disorders experience problems playing with others since many forms of play require a good understanding of the rules of social interaction, and thereby miss important social experiences (Clegg et al., 2015; Glogowska et al., 2006). Language disorders may also influence peer relations later in childhood and adolescence (Durkin and Conti-Ramsden, 2007, 2010).

Early intervention is important to prevent aberrant development and secondary effects (Fricke et al., 2013; Kaiser and Roberts, 2011). Learning a language is not primarily about the ability to point at an object or a picture when someone says a word, or to be able to pronounce words. Language is social, and it is the contexts in which words occur that lend them meaning (Nelson, 2007a). Language stimulation of children who are delayed in language development must therefore be varied and take place in a conversational setting that children are able to make sense of. Also, signing deaf children with language disorders have been found to benefit from support in their narrative development (Herman et al., 2014). All aspects of the language environment are important, not least at school where children learn "school language,"

DOI: 10.4324/9781003292524-12

that is, words and phrases related to school subjects. Children with language disorders need support to develop adequate academic and social skills. A significant percentage of children with language disorders develop **dyslexia** and may need special literacy education (see Book 4, *Cognition, Intelligence and Learning*, Chapter 38). Audiobooks, electronic books with speech output and other materials can reduce the loss of knowledge that typically results from lack of reading, and the negative consequences of poor reading skills in adulthood (Chanioti, 2017; Moe and Wright, 2013; Schiavo and Buson, 2014).

Over time, most children with early language disorders develop intelligible speech and use words and sentences in a way not readily noticed by others. Some of them, however, continue to struggle. The majority of children with distinct language disorders at the age of 7 continue to show language problems at the age of 11 (Conti-Ramsden et al., 2001). Additionally, the demands on language increase over time, although less attention is given to language development during school age (Hollands et al., 2005). Lesser cognitive and language impairments are "invisible" and can be difficult to detect without thorough assessment (Im-Bolter and Cohen, 2007). Language comprehension forms the basis for learning, and undiscovered language disorders can have a major impact on the ability to learn at school. A school environment adapted to the child's abilities can be crucial for developing language and taking full advantage of school.

In adolescence, peer conversations become more central and children with early language disorders may need language support when they reach this age (Clark et al., 2007). Research thus shows that it is essential to follow up all children with moderate or severe language disorders during preschool, when they start school, and throughout school age, even when their speech seems relatively unimpaired once they start in school. Not all children will show persistent problems, but the probability is high enough for all of them to be followed up.

Language Disorders and Emotional and Behavioral Disorders

Children with language and communication disorders experience many difficult situations. When adults meet a toddler, they typically say *hi*, ask the child for his name or say something else that requires a response from the child. When the child has delayed language, this implies focusing on the child's difficulties and may contribute to making the child more anxious in interaction with other people. Delayed language development often receives a great deal of attention in the early years, and many parents of children who struggle with language spend a lot of time trying to get their child to repeat words and sentences after them, and to name people and things. This type of "training" often has little effect and may be experienced as pressure by children. Although parents generally are positive communication partners for their children, it is better to let a professional assume the responsibility for activities that may take the form of training. Parents and others in the child's immediate environment may be guided to encourage what the child is able to do instead of focusing on the delayed development of speech. Some children develop selective mutism, meaning that they only speak at home and with their immediate family (see Book 1, *Theoretical Perspectives and Methodology*, Chapter 33), and many of them had delayed language development and speech that was difficult for others to understand when they were younger. Although they now have no problems making themselves understood, they do not talk outside the home or with children and adults outside the family (Cline and Baldwin, 2004; Scott and Beidel, 2011). Studies show that selective mutism is more frequent among children in immigrant families, reflecting that the change of language and environment implied in immigration may represent social stress for some children (Muris and Ollendick, 2015).

In addition to the many frustrating situations experienced by children with language disorders, their language problems make it difficult for them to communicate and process problematic experiences. Some react with **aggression** and by acting out, others become anxious and withdrawn; and some show both internalizing and **externalizing behavior** (Bornstein et al., 2013). Studies have found that children with language disorders have a higher incidence of mental health problems than those with normal language development, and that children with **mental disorders** have a higher incidence of language impairments (Im-Bolter and Cohen, 2007; van Daal et al., 2007). Many adolescents with **behavioral disorders** have language problems as well, especially in the social use of language (Helland et al., 2014; Lundervold et al., 2008). Research as well as clinical experience demonstrates the central role of language for mental health and the importance of including language assessment and intervention in the measures for children and adolescents with emotional and behavioral problems.

Summary

1 Communication and language distinguish human beings from other species and represent two of the main topics in developmental psychology.

2 In the second half of the first year of life, children gradually pay more attention to where others are looking. *Joint attention* means that two or more people are aware of the same thing and are aware of sharing this attention. Joint attention is independent of modality and provides a necessary foundation for the development of communicative skills and language. Children with *autism spectrum disorder* have difficulties with non-verbal communication and establishing and engaging in joint attention.

3 According to Trevarthen, *primary* and *secondary intersubjectivity* reflect an innate basis for communication. In Bloom's **intentionality** model, humans have an intrinsic motive to create and maintain *intersubjectivity*. Tomasello maintains that communication is rooted in a species-specific ability to understand and convey *intentions* and to cooperate.

4 Early *dialogues* largely take place during play or in the context of *daily routines* and involve *turn-taking* between children and adults.

5 Toward the end of the first year of life, children begin to follow *pointing* and other deictic gestures. Some theorists consider pointing to be primarily social, rooted in an innate motive to share knowledge and experiences with others. Others view pointing as a way of obtaining information and an extension of children's early exploration with their fingertips. Imitation does not seem to play a major role in the development of pointing. *Symbolic gestures* appear at the same time as children begin to say their first words and probably have their basis in children's imitation of

their parents. Gestures are never completely replaced by words and remain part of the communicative repertoire throughout life.

6 *Nativists* claim that children have an innate *language acquisition device* (LAD) in the form of a *universal grammar*. Language stimulation in itself is too "impoverished" to give rise to language, and children must therefore have an innate mechanism that perceives and processes linguistic stimulation based on a set of grammatical rules. *Behaviorism* explains language acquisition just like any other behavior as the result of conditioning and imitation. **Social constructivism** views language as a *cultural tool* that children learn to apply within a social framework. By adapting their interaction with children, adults represent a *language acquisition support system*, or **scaffolding**. *Emergentism* explains language development as the result of interaction between cognitive abilities and language experience. The language environment has "rich" enough information to allow children to learn a language. The *usage-based theory* maintains that children construct language by using it for communication; an innate predisposition is associated with communication rather than syntax and grammar. Based on current evidence, it is not possible to determine which of the theories provides the most accurate description of the language development process.

7 Children usually begin to *babble* when they approach the age of 6–7 months, and by 10 months their babbling clearly begins to absorb the sound of the surrounding language. Children learn to differentiate, recognize and produce precisely those *speech sounds that distinguish meaning* in the language(s) they grow up with.

8 Children *comprehend* some words before they begin to speak. They usually *produce* their first words around the age of 1 year, with major variation. Toward the end of the second year, their vocabulary rapidly increases. Following the *vocabulary spurt*, children learn between 5.5 and 9 new words per day.

9 The first time children hear a new word, they must *fast map* it, form an assumption about its meaning in order to recognize and use the word later. Early in development, children use words both in a broader sense (overextension) and in a narrower sense (underextension) than adults.

10 Infants spend a lot of time exploring the environment and often ask adults what things are called. Some children's early vocabulary contains many object words, while others have a more expressive

early vocabulary. Object words usually make up less than half of children's vocabulary in the second year of life. Other important word classes are verbs and adjectives. Function words are related to sentence formation and many of them are acquired relatively late. Later language development is characterized by the increasing use of *metaphors* and other *figurative language*.

11 The transition from single- to multi-word utterances is the most important **qualitative change** in language development. Children understand *multi-word utterances* before they themselves begin to produce them. Initially, children use *successive single-word utterances* that are thematically related but not linked together by an intonation contour. As inter-word pauses get progressively shorter, more words fall within the same intonation contour. *Verbs* represent an early conceptual framework for constructing sentences since they implicitly involve someone performing an action and someone or something acting as recipient. *Formulas* turn into more abstract sentence structures. *Complex sentences* are first constructed by combining sentence types that previously were expressed separately. Once children are well on their way to using sentences, they begin to *inflect* words and use function words such as *above* and *below*.

12 Conversation skills include taking initiative, responding, taking turns, clarifying misunderstandings and ending the conversation. Adults guide children's early conversations and support the child's participation. As they grow older, children's contributions become more equal and they become better at resolving misunderstandings, but they continue to have difficulty maintaining long-term focus on a single topic.

13 At an early age, children begin to construct *narratives* and share events they have experienced. The stories of younger children generally describe physical attributes, while descriptions of the characters' thoughts, feelings and motives are rare even among 5- to 6-year-olds. With age, narratives become more coherent, detailed and evaluative.

14 When adults talk to young infants and young children, they use short utterances and simple sentence structures with clear pronunciation and a somewhat lighter vocal register than in speech directed at adults. However, the characteristics of *child-directed speech* have not been found to be essential for language development. *Variation sets* in adults' language directed at young

children demonstrate that children draw on information from different sources when learning to express themselves through language.

15 Girls generally have somewhat better language skills than boys. This is particularly evident during school age, but some differences can be observed as early as preschool age. Parents speak differently to boys and to girls starting at an early age.

16 Multilingual development is common. Children with *bilingual first language acquisition* or *early second language acquisition* must learn the phonetic systems of both languages, learn which words correspond to each other in the two languages, and when to use them. Early in life, this is no more difficult than learning a single language, but children's competence in each language depends on how much it is used. Many bilingual children develop a flexibility in solving problems and thinking creatively.

17 Language can be acquired in different modalities. The development of *sign language* follows the same principles as the development of speech, although its grammar and sentence structure are quite different.

18 Some children with motor impairments, autism spectrum disorder, intellectual disability or severe language disorders have difficulty acquiring spoken language normally, even if they grow up in an adequate language environment and receive speech therapy. Intervention with manual signs and graphic symbols may give them new possibilities for communication and support their development of speech.

19 Language disorders will influence children's learning and development, whether they develop spoken language or sign language. Problems with comprehension are more critical than problems involving **expressive language** only. Children with language impairments are vulnerable to developing dyslexia. Early intervention is important and with age, most children with language disorders develop relatively inconspicuous language skills. However, some adolescents need additional language support and reduced language understanding may be a major hindrance to their academic success at school.

20 Children with language and communication disorders experience many difficult situations and are vulnerable for developing mental health problems. Children with mental disorders have a higher incidence of language disorders than other children.

Core Issues

- The emergence of communication.
- The biological and experiential bases of language.
- The functions of child-directed speech.
- The influence of non-vocal language on speech development.

Suggestions for Further Reading

Bialystok, E., Craik, F. I., Green, D. W., & Gollan, T. H. (2009). Bilingual minds. *Psychological Science in the Public Interest, 10*, 89–129.

Carpendale, J. I., & Carpendale, A. B. (2010). The development of pointing: From personal directedness to interpersonal direction. *Human Development, 53*, 110–126.

Im-Bolter N., & Cohen, N. J. (2007). Language impairment and psychiatric comorbidities. *Pediatric Clinics of North America, 54*, 525–542.

Kuhl, P. K. (2004). Early language acquisition: Cracking the speech code. *Nature Reviews Neuroscience, 5*, 831–843.

MacWhinney, B. (2004). A multiple process solution to the logical problem of language acquisition. *Journal of Child Language, 31*, 883–914.

Naber, F. B. A., Bakermans-Kranenburg, M. J., van IJzendoorn, M. H., Dietz, C., van Daalen, E., Swinkels, S. H. N., Buitelaar, J. K., & van Engeland, H. (2008). Joint attention development in toddlers with autism. *European Child and Adolescent Psychiatry, 17*, 143–152.

Tardif, T., Fletcher, P., Liang, W., Zhang, Z., Kaciroti, N., & Marchman, V. A. (2008). Baby's first 10 words. *Developmental Psychology, 44*, 929–938.

Tomasello, M. (2005). Beyond formalities: The case of language acquisition. *The Linguistic Review, 22*, 183–197.

Zevenbergen, A. A., Holmes, A., Haman, E., Whiteford, N., & Thielges, S. (2016). Variability in mothers' support for preschoolers' contributions to co-constructed narratives as a function of child age. *First Language, 36*, 601–616.

Glossary

See subject index to find the terms in the text

Adaptation   Changes that increase the ability of a species or an individual to survive and cope with the environment.

Adolescence   The period between *childhood* and adulthood, age 12–18.

Aggression   Behavior intended to harm living beings, objects or materials.

Assessment (in clinical work)   The mapping of an individual's strengths and weaknesses, competencies and problem areas.

Atypical development   Course of development that differs significantly from the development of the majority of a *population*; see *individual differences* and *typical development*.

Augmentative and alternative communication   Non-vocal communication methods that can replace and supplement the functions of speech.

Autism spectrum disorder   Neurodevelopmental disorder that appears in the first years of life; characterized by persistent deficits in social skills, communication and language, and by repetitive behavior and restricted interests.

Autobiographical memory   Memory of chronologically organized sequences of personally experienced events.

Babbling   Speech-like vocalization; usually occurs at 6–7 months of age.

Behavioral disorder   All forms of behavior that are socially unacceptable in one way or another, such as running away from home, screaming, cursing, messy eating manners, bed-wetting, ritual behavior, excessive dependency, poor *emotion regulation*, *aggression*, fighting and *bullying*.

Behaviorism; Behavior analysis   Group of psychological theories that emphasize the influence of the environment to explain developmental changes.

Checklist   Questionnaire or interview with specific observational categories, questions or statements answered by an individual respondent or by others; often used to assess the development of an individual in one or more areas.

Childhood   Age 1–12 years.

Child-directed speech   Adults' and older children's adaptation of pitch, *intonation* and *syntax* when talking to infants and toddlers.

Cognition   Thinking or understanding; includes some type of perception of the world, storage in the form of mental *representation*, different ways of managing or processing new and stored experiences, and action strategies.

Communication   Intentional conveyance of thoughts, stories, desires, ideas, emotions, etc., to one or more persons.

Communicative intention   Intention to convey a thought or an idea, direct others' attention at ideas or conditions in the outside world, or get others to do something specific; see *communication*.

Conditioning   The learning of a specific reaction in response to specific stimuli; includes classical and operant conditioning. In *classical conditioning*, a neutral stimulus is associated with an unlearned or *unconditioned stimulus* that elicits an unlearned or *unconditioned response*, eventually transforming the neutral stimulus into a conditioned stimulus that elicits a conditioned response similar to the unconditioned response. In *operant conditioning*, an action is followed by an event that increases or reduces the probability that the action will be repeated under similar circumstances; see *reinforcement*.

Connectionism   Theory within the information-processing tradition; based on a model of mental functioning by which external stimulation leads to various activating and inhibitory processes that may occur sequentially (following one another in time) or in parallel (simultaneously); knowledge is represented as a pattern of activation and inhibition, and new networks give rise to phenomena that differ qualitatively from the processes from which they emerged; see also *emergentism*.

Constraint (in development)   The organism's resistance to change and adaptation to new experiences; often used in connection with the nervous system.

Constructivism Psychological theories based on the notion that an individual constructs his or her understanding of the outside world; see *social constructivism*.

Contrast principle (in language development) Refers to children's assumption that every new word has a different meaning from the words they have previously learned.

Control group Group of individuals that is compared with an *experimental group* as similar to the control group as possible in relevant areas, but not exposed to the experimental variable.

Correlation Measure of the degree of covariation between two variables, ranging from −1.00 to +1.00; values close to 0.00 show a low degree of correlation; a positive correlation (+) means that a high score on one variable is associated with high score on the other; a negative correlation (−) indicates that a high score on one variable is associated with a low score on the other.

Cultural tool According to Vygotsky, a skill that has developed through generations in a culture, and that is passed on to children, such as language, the numerical system or calendar time.

Culture The particular activities, tools, attitudes, beliefs, values, norms, etc., that characterize a group or a community.

Declarative communication Form of communication with the sole purpose of providing information and directing someone else's attention at something, such as a person, an object or an idea; see *instrumental communication*.

Deictic gesture Pointing gesture; gesture that directs others' attention at something in the environment without naming it.

Development Changes over time in the structure and functioning of human beings and animals as a result of interaction between biological and environmental factors.

Developmental disorder Disorder that is congenital or appears in *infancy* or *childhood* without the presence of external injuries or similar.

Diary Study (in research on children) Research method based on parents' written record of their child's actions or utterances.

Disability The difference between an individual's abilities and the demands of the environment.

Dishabituation Increased response to a new stimulus or aspect of a stimulus following a reduction in response intensity due to repeated presentation of a stimulus; see *habituation*.

Domain A delimited sphere of knowledge; an area in which something is active or manifests itself.

Down syndrome; Trisomy 21 Syndrome that causes varying degrees of *intellectual disability*; caused by an error in cell division that results in a partial or complete extra copy of chromosome 21.

Dyslexia Severe reading and writing disorder, despite adequate sensory and intellectual abilities and appropriate training.

Emergentism Theoretical approach related to *connectionism*; based on the premise that existing elements and processes interact to give rise to new phenomena that are qualitatively different from the elements and processes they emerged from.

Enculturation Acquisition of a culture's practices, customs, norms, values, and the like; the first foundation in this process is children's innate social orientation.

Executive functions Cognitive functions that monitor and regulate attention and plan and supervise the execution of voluntary actions, including the inhibition to act on inappropriate impulses.

Expansion (in language development) The repetition of what a child is saying by an adult, with longer sentences and greater complexity.

Experiment Method to test a hypothesis on specific causal relationships or connections. One or several conditions are systematically altered, and the effect is recorded. As many conditions as possible are kept constant in order not to affect the outcome, increasing the probability that the results are solely related to the conditions being studied.

Experimental group In experiments with two groups, the group that receives the experimental treatment or other influence; see *control group*.

Exploration According to Bowlby, a behavioral system whose function is to provide information about the environment and enable the individual to better adapt to it; activated by unfamiliar and/or complex objects; deactivated once the objects have been examined and become familiar to the individual.

Expressive language The language that the child produces.

Extension (of a concept) All actual and possible exemplars encompassed by a concept.

Externalizing disorder Negative emotions directed at others; often expressed in the form of antisocial and aggressive behavior.

Figurative language Language that makes use of metaphors or similes to express facts or ideas; see *metaphor*.

Gender difference; Sex difference Characteristic, ability or behavior pattern that differs between the two sexes.

Gesture Distinct movement primarily used as a means of communication and interpreted consistently within a social system; see *deictic gesture* and *symbolic gesture*.

Grammar Rules that describe how sentences are formed in a language; includes *morphology* and *syntax*.

Habituation Gradual reduction in the intensity of a reaction or response following repeated stimulation; allows an individual to ignore familiar objects and direct attention at new ones.

Imitation The deliberate execution of an action to create a correspondence between what oneself does and what someone else does.

Imperative communication See *instrumental communication*.

Incidence The appearance of new occurrences of a trait, disease or similar in a particular *population* during a particular time span, often expressed as the number of incidences per 1,000 individuals per year.

Individual differences Variation in skills and characteristics between the individuals in a *population*; see *atypical development* and *typical development*.

Infancy The first year of life.

Information processing (theory) Psychological theories based on the assumption that all mental phenomena can be described and explained by models in which the flow of information is processed by one or more systems.

Instinct Species-specific behavior with a genetic basis, such as nest-building among birds.

Instrumental communication Communicative action aimed at getting someone else to do something specific; see *declarative communication*.

Intellectual disability; Learning disability; Mental retardation Significant problems learning and adjusting that affect most areas of functioning; graded mild (IQ 70–50), moderate (IQ 49–35), severe (IQ 34–20) and profound (IQ below 20); in clinical contexts, a significant reduction in social adjustment is an additional criterion.

Intentionality   Goal-oriented determination; includes a notion of the goal of an action, and emotions and plans related to achieving the goal.

Internalization   Process whereby external processes are reconstructed to become internal processes, such as when children independently adopt problem-solving strategies they have previously used in interaction with others, or adopt the attitudes, characteristics and standards of others as their own.

Intersubjectivity   The consciously shared subjective experience of an event or phenomenon by two or more individuals simultaneously.

Intonation   The melody or pattern of changes in the pitch of the speaking voice.

Joint attention   Two or more individuals share a common focus of attention, while at the same time being aware that the same focus of attention is shared by the other person(s).

Language Acquisition Device, LAD   According to Chomsky, an innate grammatical representation, a *module* for language that underlies all languages and enables children to learn to understand the language around them and assemble words into grammatically correct phrases.

Language Acquisition Support System, LASS   According to Bruner, the systematic way in which the environment supports a child's language development; see *scaffold*.

Learning   Relatively permanent change in understanding and behavior as the result of experience; see *development*.

Lexical development   The development of vocabulary.

Mental disorder   Behavioral or psychological pattern that occurs in an individual and leads to clinically significant distress or impairment in one or more important areas of functioning.

Metaphor   A type of *analogy*; meaning expressed illustratively or figuratively.

Minority language   Language spoken by a minority of a society's population.

Module (in cognition)   Isolated brain system that deals with a particular type of stimulation and knowledge.

Morphology   The study of how words are built up; includes the creation of content words like *ball* and *run*, functional words like *and* and *in*, and inflections of word forms like *run*, *ran* and *running*.

Multilingualism   Proficiency in two or more languages at roughly the same level, with bilingualism being the most common form. Multilingualism may be practiced within the family alone, or between the family and society; see *minority language*.

Nativism   Theoretical assumption that development proceeds according to a plan that in some way is represented genetically, and that experience has little or no effect on the developmental outcome.

Overextension   Use of a word beyond its usual meaning; see *under-extension*.

Perception   Knowledge gained through the senses; discernment, selection and processing of sensory input.

Personality   An individual's characteristic tendency to feel, think and act in specific ways.

Personality traits   Summary description of an individual's *personality*.

Phoneme   The smallest unit of sound that distinguishes two words in a language; /m/ and /p/, for example, are different phonemes in English, since *mile* and *pile* are different English words.

Phonology   Branch of linguistics dealing with the sounds of spoken language.

Pragmatics (in language)   Functions of language in everyday use.

Prelinguistic   Refers to children's skills and abilities before they begin to speak, for example prelinguistic *communication*.

Preschool age   Age 3–6 years.

Primary intersubjectivity   According to Trevarthen, younger infants' perception of how they affect others, and the fact that others are aware of them; see *secondary intersubjectivity*.

Private speech   Speech that does not convey enough information to allow the listener to understand what is being communicated.

Qualitative change   Change in the nature or quality of a phenomenon.

Recognition   The process of experiencing something in the moment that has been experienced before, such as when children consciously or nonconsciously show that they have seen a particular image before.

Referential communication   Use of language that enables the other person to identify a particular individual, object or event in the current environment.

Referential style (in early language development)   According-ing to Nelson, speech characterized by a preponderance of words referring to objects.

Reinforcement (in conditioning)   In *classical conditioning*: presentation of an *unconditioned stimulus* and a *neutral stimulus* that becomes a *conditioned stimulus*, such that the *conditioned response* is triggered more consistently. In *operant conditioning*: events that follow the execution of an action and increase the likelihood of repeating the action under similar circumstances.

Representation (mental)   An individual's mental storage of understanding and knowledge about the world.

Ritualization   Process whereby involuntary forms of expression, such as facial expressions, evolve into *signals*; or a process whereby a voluntary action becomes a communicative *gesture*, for example when a reaching movement turns into a pointing gesture.

Scaffold; scaffolding   In *social constructivism*, the external regulation, help and support provided by adults or more experienced peers to children, adapted to their level and allowing them to transcend their independent coping skills and develop new skills and knowledge.

School age   Age 6–12.

Secondary intersubjectivity   According to Trevarthen, the *joint attention* of children and adults on something outside themselves, as well as their awareness of each other's attention.

Self   Personal awareness, perception or evaluation of oneself.

Self-disclosure   Communicating personal information about oneself to others; typical in *adolescence*.

Self-image   Positive or negative perception of oneself and one's own characteristics.

Self-regulation   The ability to monitor and adapt one's own thoughts, feelings, reactions and actions in order to cope with the requirements, challenges and opportunities of the environment and be able to achieve one's goals; also referred to as self-control.

Sensory modality   One of several specific senses, such as vision or hearing.

Sex   See *gender difference*.

Shaping (of behavior)   Step-by-step *reinforcement* of behavior in such a way that it gradually changes and increasingly resembles desired behavior; part of *operant conditioning*.

Sign language Visual-manual language, primarily using movements of the arms, hands and fingers, supported by body movements, mouth movements and facial gestures.

Signals (in early development) Infant actions and expressions used by adults as an indication of the infant's interests, preferences and general well-being.

Social constructivism Psychological theories based on the notion that children construct their understanding of the outside world through interaction and cooperation with other people, and that people in different cultures (including the subcultures of a society) can perceive one and the same phenomenon in different ways.

Social mediation Social communication of or guidance toward knowledge.

Socioeconomic status (SES) Assessment of an individual's economic and social status in society; for children, usually based on information about the parents' education and occupation.

Stability (in development) Describes the constancy of an individual's position in relation to peers with respect to a particular characteristic; the fact that individual differences in the execution of a skill are constant from one developmental stage to another.

Stage (in development) Delimited period of time in which thoughts, feelings and behavior are organized in a way that is qualitatively different from the preceding or following periods.

Successive one-word utterances Utterances during early language development that consist of several thematically related words, but articulated in such a way that the words do not lie within the same intonation contour, but have short pauses between them; see *intonation*.

Symbol Something that represents something other than itself, such as a sign, a word, an image or the like.

Symbolic gesture Gesture that specifies or names the thing or category it refers to; see *deictic gesture*.

Syndrome Set of attributes and behavioral characteristics that regularly occur together.

Syntax The grammatical arrangement of words and phrases in a language.

Test Measurement instrument; a collection of questions or tasks that provide a basis for assessing an individual's performance relative to peers or a specific set of criteria.

Toddlerhood Age 1–3.

Typical development Course of development that characterizes the majority of a *population*; see *atypical development* and *individual differences*.

Underextension Use of a word more limited than its usual meaning; see *over-extension*.

Universal grammar In Chomsky's theory, an innate grammatical device that contains the grammars of all human languages.

Variation set A set of statements that express the same information in slightly different ways; common in *child-directed speech*.

Vocable Vocalization of a speech-like sound without conventional meaning in the child's language environment; typically occurs during early language development.

Vocabulary spurt A rapid increase in productive vocabulary that typically characterizes children's language from the end of the second year of life; often defined as the first month in which a child's vocabulary increases by 15 words or more, often coinciding with the child's earliest two-word utterances.

Vulnerability An individual's susceptibility to be adversely affected by particular conditions or circumstances in the environment.

Williams syndrome Genetic syndrome characterized by heart defects, distinctive facial features, a short stature, developmental delays in the fetal stage and later, problems thriving during *infancy*, mild or moderate *learning disabilities*, good language abilities compared with other skills, and trusting behavior toward other people.

Bibliography

Abrahamsen, E. P., & Smith, R. (2000). Facilitating idiom acquisition in children with communication disorders: Computer vs classroom. *Child Language Teaching and Therapy, 16*, 227–239.

Acredolo, L. P., & Goodwyn, S. (2009). *Baby signs: How to talk with your baby before your baby can talk, Third edition.* New York, NY: McGraw Hill.

Allan, K. (1977). Classifiers. *Language, 53*, 285–311.

Altınkamış, N. F., Kern, S., & Sofu, H. (2014). When context matters more than language: Verb or noun in French and Turkish caregiver speech. *First Language, 34*, 537–550.

Ambridge, B., & Lieven, E. V. M. (2011). *Child language acquisition: Contrasting theoretical approaches.* Cambridge: Cambridge University Press.

Andersen, E. S. (1990). *Speaking with style. The sociolinguistic skills of children.* London: Routledge.

Anglin, J. M. (1993). Knowing versus learning words. *Monographs of the Society for Research in Child Development, 58*, 10.

Asch, S., & Nerlove, H. (1960). The development of double function terms in children: An exploratory investigation. In B. Kaplan & S. Wapner (Eds), *Perspectives in psychological theory: Essays in honor of Heinz Werner* (pp. 47–60). New York, NY: International Universities Press.

Aubusson, P. J., Harrison, A. G., & Ritchie, S. M. (Eds) (2006). *Metaphor and analogy in science education.* Dordrecht, NL: Springer.

Baixauli, I., Colomer, C., Roselló, B., & Miranda, A. (2016). Narratives of children with high-functioning autism spectrum disorder: A meta-analysis. *Research in Developmental Disabilities, 59*, 234–254.

Bannard, C., & Lieven, E. (2012). Formulaic language in L1 acquisition. *Annual Review of Applied Linguistics, 32*, 3–16.

Barnes-Holmes, Y., Hayes, S. C., Barnes-Holmes, Y., & Roche, B. (2001). Relational frame theory. Post-Skinnerian account of human language and cognition. *Advances in Child Development and Behavior, 28*, 101–138.

Barrett, M., Harris, M., & Chasin, J. (1991). Early lexical development and maternal speech: A comparison of children's initial and subsequent uses of words. *Journal of Child Language, 18,* 21–40.

Bates, E., Dale, P. S., & Thal, D. (1995). Individual differences and their implications for theories of language development. In P. Fletcher & B. MacWhinney (Eds), *Handbook of child language* (pp. 96–151). Oxford: Basil Blackwell.

Begeer, S., Dik, M., Marieke, J., Asbrock, D., Brambring, M., & Kef, S. (2014). A new look at theory of mind in children with ocular and ocular-plus congenital blindness. *Journal of Visual Impairment and Blindness, 108,* 17–27.

Berman, R. A. (2007). Developing linguistic knowledge and language use across adolescence. In E. Hoff & M. Shatz (Eds), *Blackwell handbook of language development* (pp. 347–367). Oxford: Blackwell.

Bialystok, E. (2001). *Bilingualism in development: Language, literacy, and cognition.* New York, NY: Cambridge University Press.

Bialystok, E., & Luk, G. (2012). Receptive vocabulary differences in monolingual and bilingual adults. *Bilingualism: Language and Cognition, 15,* 397–401.

Bialystok, E., Craik, F. I., & Luk, G. (2012). Bilingualism: Consequences for mind and brain. *Trends in Cognitive Sciences, 16,* 240–250.

Bigelow, A. (2003). The development of joint attention in blind children. *Development and Psychopathology, 15,* 259–275

Bishop, D. V. M. (2006). What causes specific language impairment in children? *Current Directions in Psychological Science, 15,* 217–221.

Bjerkan, B., Martinsen, H., Schjølberg, S., & von Tetzchner, S. (1983, July). *Communicative development and adult reactions.* Presented at 2nd International Conference on Social Pychology and Language, Bristol.

Bloom, L. (1973). *One word at a time.* The Hague, NL: Mouton.

Bloom, L. (1993). *The transition from infancy to language: Acquiring the power of expression.* Cambridge: Cambridge University Press.

Bloom, L. (1998). Language acquisition in its developmental context. In W. Damon, D. Kuhn & R. S. Siegler (Eds), *Handbook of child psychology, Fifth edition, Volume 2: Cognition, perception and language* (pp. 309–370). New York, NY: John Wiley.

Bloom, P. (2004). Myths of word learning. In D. G. Hall & S. R. Waxman (Eds), *Weaving a lexicon* (pp. 205–220). Cambridge, MA: MIT Press.

Bondy, A., & Frost, L. (2002). *A picture's worth: PECS and other visual communication strategies in autism.* Bethesda, MD: Woodbine House.

Bornstein, M. H., Hahn, C. S., & Suwalsky, J. T. (2013). Developmental pathways among adaptive functioning and externalizing and internalizing behavioral problems: Cascades from childhood into adolescence. *Applied Developmental Science, 7,* 76–87.

Bornstein, M. H., Cote, L. R., Maital, S., Painter, K., Park, S. Y., Pascual, L., Pêcheux, M. G., Ruel, J., Venuti, P., & Vyt, A. (2004). Cross-linguistic analysis of vocabulary in young children: Spanish, Dutch, French, Hebrew, Italian, Korean, and American English. *Child Development, 75,* 1115–1139.

Boucher, J. (2012). Research review: Structural language in autistic spectrum disorder – characteristics and causes. *Journal of Child Psychology and Psychiatry*, *53*, 219–233.

Bowerman, M., & Choi, S. (2001). Shaping meanings for language: Universal and language-specific in the acquisition and shaping of semantic categories. In M. Bowerman & S. Levinson (Eds), *Language acquisition and conceptual development* (pp. 475–511). Cambridge: Cambridge University Press.

Braine, M. D. S. (1994). Is nativism sufficient? *Journal of Child Language*, *21*, 9–31.

Brodsky, P., Waterfall, H. R., & Edelman, S. (2007). Characterising motherese: On the computational; structure of child-directed language. In D. S. McNamara & J. G. Trafton (Eds), *Proceedings of the 29th Annual Cognitive Science Society* (pp. 833–838). Austin, TX: Cognitive Science Society.

Brown, R. (1958). *Words and things*. New York, NY: Free Press.

Bruner, J. S. (1975). The ontogenesis of speech acts. *Journal of Child Language*, *2*, 1–19.

Bruner, J. S. (1983). *Child's talk*. Oxford: Oxford University Press.

Bruner, J. S. (1991). The narrative construction of reality. *Critical Inquiry*, *18*, 1–21.

Butterworth, G. (2003). Pointing is the royal road to language for babies. In S. Kita (Ed.), *Pointing: Where language, culture, and cognition meet* (pp. 9–33). Mahwah, NJ: Lawrence Erlbaum.

Camaioni, L., Perucchini, P., Muratori, F., Parrini, B., & Cesari, A. (2003). The communicative use of pointing in autism: Developmental profile and factors related to change. *European Psychiatry*, *18*, 6–12.

Cameron-Faulkner, T., Lieven, E., & Tomasello, M. (2003). A construction based analysis of child directed speech. *Cognitive Science*, *27*, 843–873.

Campbell, R. N. (1986). Language acquisition and cognition. In P. Fletcher & M. Garman (Eds), *Language acquisition, Second edition* (pp. 30–48). Cambridge: Cambridge University Press.

Carey, S. (1978). The child as word learner. In M. Halle, J. Bresnan & G. A. Miller (Eds), *Linguistic theory and psychological reality* (pp. 264–293). Cambridge, MA: MIT Press.

Carpendale, J. I. M., & Carpendale, A. B. (2010). The development of pointing: From personal directedness to interpersonal direction. *Human Development*, *53*, 110–126.

Carpenter, M., & Liebal, K. (2011). Joint attention, communication, and knowing together in infancy. In A. Seemann (Ed.), *Joint attention: New developments in psychology, philosophy of mind, and social neuroscience* (pp. 159–181). Cambridge, MA: The MIT Press.

Chahboun, S., Vulchanov, V., Saldaña, D., Eshuis, H., & Vulchanova, M. (2016). Can you play with fire and not hurt yourself? A comparative study in figurative language comprehension between individuals with and without autism spectrum disorder. *PloS one*, *11* (*12*), e0168571.

Chang, F., Dell, G. S., & Bock, K. (2006). Becoming syntactic. *Psychological Review, 113,* 234–272.

Chang, Y. C., Shire, S. Y., Shih, W., Gelfand, C., & Kasari, C. (2016). Preschool deployment of evidence-based social communication intervention: JASPER in the classroom. *Journal of Autism and Developmental Disorders, 46,* 2211–2223.

Chanioti, E. (2017). Dyslexia in primary school: A new platform for identifying reading errors and improving reading skills. In P. Anastasiades & N. Zaranis (Eds), *Research on e-learning and ICT in education* (pp. 257–271). Cham, Switzerland; Springer.

Chomsky, N. (1959). Review of Skinner's Verbal Behavior. *Language, 35,* 26–58.

Chomsky, N. (1968). *Language and mind.* New York: Harcourt Brace Jovanovich.

Chomsky, N. (1986). *Knowledge of language: Its nature, origin, and use.* London: Praeger.

Chomsky, N. (2000). *New horizons in the study of language and mind.* Cambridge: Cambridge University Press.

Chouinard, M. M., & Clark, E. V. (2003). Adult reformulations of child errors as negative evidence. *Journal of Child Language, 30,* 637–669.

Christiansen, M. H., & Chater, N. (2008). Language as shaped by the brain. *Behavioral and Brain Sciences, 31,* 489–558.

Clark, A., O'Hare, A., Watson, J., Cohen, W., Cowie, H., Elton, R., Nasir, J., & Seckl, J. (2007). Severe receptive language disorder in childhood—familial aspects and long-term outcomes: Results from a Scottish study. *Archives of Disease in Childhood, 92,* 614–619.

Clark, E. V. (1981). Lexical innovations: How children learn to create new words. In W. Deutsch (Ed.), *The child's construction of language* (pp. 299–328). London: Academic Press.

Clark, E. V. (1992). Conventionality and contrast: Pragmatic principles with lexical consequences. In A. Lehrer & E. F. Kittay (Eds), *Frames, fields and contrasts* (pp. 171–188). Hove, UK: Lawrence Erlbaum.

Clark, E. V. (2016). *First language acquisition, Third edition.* Cambridge: Cambridge University Press.

Cleave, P. L., Becker, S. D., Curran, M. K., Van Horne, A. J. O., & Fey, M. E. (2015). The efficacy of recasts in language intervention: A systematic review and meta-analysis. *American Journal of Speech-Language Pathology, 24,* 237–255.

Clegg, J., Law, J., Rush, R., Peters, T. J., & Roulstone, S. (2015). The contribution of early language development to children's emotional and behavioural functioning at 6 years: An analysis of data from the Children in Focus sample from the ALSPAC birth cohort. *Journal of Child Psychology and Psychiatry, 56,* 67–75.

Clibbens, J. (2001). Signing and lexical development in children with Down syndrome. *Down Syndrome Research and Practice, 7,* 101–105.

Cline, T., & Baldwin, S. (2004). *Selective mutism in children, Second edition*. London: Whurr/Wiley.

Collier, K., Bickel, B., van Schaik, C. P., Manser, M. B., & Townsend, S. W. (2014). Language evolution: Syntax before phonology? *Proceedings of the Royal Society B: Biological Sciences, 281,* 20140263.

Collis, G. M., & Schaffer, H. R. (1975). Synchronization of visual attention in mother–infant pairs. *Journal of Child Psychology and Psychiatry, 16,* 315–320.

Conti-Ramsden, G., Botting, N., Simkin, Z., & Knox, E. (2001). Follow-up of children attending infant language units: Outcomes at 11 years of age. *International Journal of Language and Communication Disorders, 36,* 207–219.

Coppola, M. (2002). *The emergence of the grammatical category of Subject in home sign: Evidence from family-based gesture systems in Nicaragua*. Doctoral Dissertation, University of Rochester, USA.

Csibra, G. (2010). Recognizing communicative intentions in infancy. *Mind and Language, 25,* 141–168.

De Houwer, A. (2009). *Bilingual first language acquisition*. Bristol, UK: Multilingual Matters.

De Houwer, A. (2013). Harmonious bilingual development: Young families' well-being in language contact situations. *International Journal of Bilingualism, 19,* 169–184.

de Saussure, F. (1974). *Course in general linguistics*. Glasgow: Collins.

Dekker, T. M., & Karmiloff-Smith, A. (2011). The dynamics of ontogeny: A neuroconstructivist perspective on genes, brains, cognition and behavior. *Progress in Brain Research, 189,* 23–33.

Derwing, B. L., & Baker, W. J. (1986). Assessing morphological development. In P. Fletcher & M. Garman (Eds), *Language acquisition, Second edition* (pp. 326–338). Cambridge: Cambridge University Press.

Desrochers, S., Morisette, P., & Richard, M. (1995). Two perspectives on pointing in infancy. In C. Moore & P. J. Dunham (Eds), *Joint attention: Its origins and role in development* (pp. 85–101). Hillsdale, NJ: Erlbaum.

Dodd, B. (1975). Children's understanding of their own phonological forms. *Quarterly Journal of Experimental Psychology, 27,* 165–172.

Dollaghan, C. (1985). Child meets word: "Fast mapping" in preschool children. *Journal of Speech and Hearing Research, 28,* 449–454.

Dore, J. (1977). "Oh them sheriff": A pragmatic analysis of children's responses to questions. In S. Ervin Tripp & C. Mitchell-Kernan (Eds), *Child Discourse* (pp. 139–163). New York, NY: Academic Press.

Dore, J. (1986). The development of conversational competence. In R. L. Schiefelbusch (Ed.), *Language competence: Assessment and intervention* (pp. 3–60). London: Taylor and Francis.

Drager, K., Light, J., & McNaughton, D. (2010). Effects of AAC interventions on communication and language for young children with complex communication needs. *Journal of Pediatric Rehabilitation Medicine, 3 (4),* 303–310.

Dromi, E. (1993). The mysteries of early lexical development: Underlying cognitive and linguistic processes in meaning acquisition. In E. Dromi (Ed.), *Language and cognition: A developmental perspective* (pp. 32–60). Norwood, NJ: Ablex.

Durand, V. M., & Merges, E. (2001). Functional communication training: A contemporary behavior analytic intervention for problem behaviors. *Focus on Autism and Other Developmental Disabilities, 16,* 110–119.

Durkin, K., & Conti-Ramsden, G. (2007). Language, social behavior, and the quality of friendships in adolescents with and without a history of specific language impairment. *Child Development, 78,* 1441–1457.

Ebert, K. D., Kohnert, K., Pham, G., Disher, J. R., & Payesteh, B. (2014). Three treatments for bilingual children with primary language impairment: Examining cross-linguistic and cross-domain effects. *Journal of Speech, Language, and Hearing Research, 57,* 172–186.

Eimas, P. D. (1985). The perception of speech in early infancy. *Scientific American, 252, 46–52,* 120.

Elman, J. L., Bates, E. A., Johnson, M. H., Karmiloff-Smith, A., Parisi, D., & Plunkett, K. (1996). *Rethinking innateness. A connectionist perspective on development.* London: MIT Press.

Erickson, L. C., & Thiessen, E. D. (2015). Statistical learning of language: Theory, validity, and predictions of a statistical learning account of language acquisition. *Developmental Review, 37,* 66–108.

Evans, V. (2014). *The language myth: Why language is not an instinct.* Cambridge: Cambridge University Press.

Fagan, M. K. (2015). Why repetition? Repetitive babbling, auditory feedback, and cochlear implantation. *Journal of Experimental Child Psychology, 137,* 125–136.

Ferguson, C. A. (1978). Learning to pronounce: The earliest stages of phonological development in the child. In F. D. Minifie & L. L. Lloyd (Eds), *Communicative and cognitive abilities – Early behavioral assessment* (pp. 273–297). Baltimore, MD: University Park Press.

Fernald, A., & Mazzie, C. (1991). Prosody and focus in speech to infants and adults. *Developmental Psychology, 27,* 209–221.

Fivush, R., Sales, J. M., & Bohanek, J. G. (2008). Meaning making in mothers' and children's narratives of emotional events. *Memory, 16,* 579–594

Fraiberg, S. (1977). *Insights from the blind.* New York, NY: Basic Books.

Franco, F., & Butterworth, G. (1996). Pointing and social awareness: Declaring and requesting in the second year. *Journal of Child Language, 23,* 307–336.

Fricke, S., Bowyer-Crane, C., Haley, A. J., Hulme, C., & Snowling, M. J. (2013). Efficacy of language intervention in the early years. *Journal of Child Psychology and Psychiatry, 54,* 280–290.

Gathercole, V. C. (1987). The contrastive hypothesis for the acquisition of word meaning: A reconsideration of the theory. *Journal of Child Language, 14,* 493–531.

Genese, F., & Nicoladis, E. (2007). Bilingual first language development. In E. Hoff & M. Shatz (Eds), *Handbook of child language development* (pp. 324–342). Oxford: Blackwell.

Gentner, D., & Bowerman, M. (2009). Why some spatial semantic categories are harder to learn than others: The typological prevalence hypothesis. In J. Guo, E. Lieven, N. Budwig, S. Ervin-Tripp, K. Nakamura & S. Özcaliskan, (Eds), *Crosslinguistic approaches to the psychology of language: Research in the tradition of Dan Isaac Slobin* (pp. 465–480). New York, NY: Psychology Press.

Gillam, R. B., & Pearson, N. (2004). *Test of narrative language*. Austin, TX: Pro-Ed.

Gleason, J. B., & Greif, E. (1983). Men's speech to young children. In B. Thorne, C. Kraemerae & N. Henley (Eds), *Language, gender and society* (pp. 140–150). Rowley, MA: Newbury House.

Gleason, J. B., Phillips, B. C., Ely, R., & Zaretsky, E. (2009). Alligators all around: The acquisition of animal terms in English and Russian. In J. Guo, E. Lieven, N. Budwig, S. Ervin-Tripp, K. Nakamura & S. Özcaliskan (Eds), *Crosslinguistic approaches to the psychology of language: Research in the tradition of Dan Isaac Slobin* (pp. 17–26). New York, NY: Psychology Press.

Glogowska, M., Roulstone, S., Peters, T. J., & Enderby, P. (2006). Early speech- and language-impaired children: Linguistic, literacy and social outcomes. *Developmental Medicine and Child Neurology, 48,* 489–494.

Glucksberg, S., Krauss, R. M., & Weisberg, R. (1966). Referential communication in nursery school children: Method and some preliminary findings. *Journal of Experimental Child Psychology, 3,* 333–342.

Goldin-Meadow, S. (2015). Gesture and cognitive development. In R. M. Lerner, L. Liben & U. Muller (Eds), *Handbook of child psychology and developmental science, Seventh edition, Volume 2: Cognitive processes* (pp. 339–380). New York, NY: Wiley.

Goldstein, M. H., & West, M. J. (1999). Consistent responses of human mothers to prelinguistic infants: The effect of prelinguistic repertoire size. *Journal of Comparative Psychology, 113,* 52–58.

Golinkoff, R. M., Hirsh-Pasek, K., Mervis, C. B., Frawley, W. B., & Parillo, M. (1995). Lexical principles can be extended to the acquisition of verbs. In M. Tomasello & W. E. Merriman (Eds), *Beyond names for things: Young children's acquisition of verbs* (pp. 185–221). Hillsdale, NJ: Erlbaum.

Gopnik, A., & Choi, S. (1995). Names, relational words, and cognitive development in English and Korean speakers: Nouns are not always learned before verbs. In M. Tomasello & W. E. Merriman (Eds), *Beyond names for things: Young children's acquisition of verbs* (pp. 63–80). Hillsdale, NJ: Erlbaum.

Greer, R. D., & Keohane, D. D. (2005). The evolution of verbal behavior in children. *Behavioral Development Bulletin, 12,* 31–47.

Griffiths, P. (1986). Early vocabulary. In P. Fletcher & M. Garman (Eds), *Language acquisition, Second edition* (pp. 279–306). Cambridge: Cambridge University Press.

Grosjean, F. (1982). *Life with two languages: An introduction to bilingualism.* Cambridge, MA: Harvard University Press.

Grosjean, F. (2010). *Bilingual.* Cambridge, MA: Harvard University Press.

Habermas, T., & de Silveira, C. (2008). The development of global coherence in life narratives across adolescence: Temporal, causal, and thematic aspects. *Developmental Psychology, 44,* 707–721.

Håkansson, G., & Westander, J. (2013). *Communication in humans and other animals.* Amsterdam: John Benjamins.

Hansegård, N. E. (1968). *Tvåspråkighet eller halvspråkighet?* Stockholm, Sweden: Aldas.

Happé, F. G. E. (1995). Understanding minds and metaphors: Insights from the study of figurative language in autism. *Metaphor and Symbolic Activity, 10,* 275–295.

Harris, M. (1992). *Language experience and early language development: From input to uptake.* London: Erlbaum.

Hart, B., & Risley, T. R. (1992). American parenting of language learning children: Persisting differences in family – child interactions observed in natural home environments. *Developmental Psychology, 28,* 1096–1105.

Helland, W. A., Lundervold, A. J., Heimann, M., & Posserud, M. B. (2014). Stable associations between behavioral problems and language impairments across childhood – The importance of pragmatic language problems. *Research in Developmental Disabilities, 35,* 943–951.

Herman, L. M. (2010). What laboratory research has told us about dolphin cognition. *International Journal of Comparative Psychology, 23,* 310–330.

Herman, R., Rowley, K., Mason, K., & Morgan, G. (2014). Deficits in narrative abilities in child British Sign Language users with specific language impairment. *International Journal of Language and Communication Disorders, 49,* 343–353.

Herrmann, E., Call, J., Hernandez-Lloreda, M., Hare, B., & Tomasello, M. (2007). Humans have evolved specialized skills of social cognition: The cultural intelligence hypothesis. *Science, 317,* 1360–1366.

Hoff, E. (2006). How social contexts support and shape language development. *Developmental Review, 26,* 55–88.

Hoff, E. (2013). Interpreting the early language trajectories of children from low-SES and language minority homes: Implications for closing achievement gaps. *Developmental psychology, 49,* 4–14.

Hoff, E., Core, C., Place, S., Rumiche, R., Señor, M., & Parra, M. (2012). Dual language exposure and early bilingual development. *Journal of Child Language, 39,* 1–27.

Hoff-Ginsberg, E. (1990). Maternal speech and the child's development of syntax: A further look. *Journal of Child Language, 17,* 85–99.

Hoiting, N. (2006). *Growing attention: From getting attention to signing variation sets.* Presented at the 8th Oslo Workshop on early Attention, Interaction and Communication, University of Oslo, October 24th, 2006.

Hollands, K., van Kraayenoord, C. E., & McMahon, S. (2005). Support to adolescents experiencing language difficulties: A survey of speech-language pathologists. *International Journal of Speech-Language Pathology, 7*, 113–129.

Hollich, G. J., Hirsh-Pasek, K., Golinkoff, R. M., Brand, R. J., Brown, E., Chung, H. L., Hennon, E., Rocroi, C., & Bloom, L. (2000). Breaking the language barrier: An emergentist coalition model for the origins of word learning. *Monographs of the Society for Research in Child Development, 65*, 3.

Hughes-Scholes, C. H., & Gavidia-Payne, S. (2016). Development of a routines-based early childhood intervention model. *Educar em Revista, 59*, 141–154.

Im-Bolter, N., & Cohen, N. J. (2007). Language impairment and psychiatric comorbidities. *Pediatric Clinics of North America, 54*, 525–542.

Inhelder, B., & Piaget, J. (1964). *The early growth of logic in the child: Classification and seriation*. London: Routledge and Kegan Paul.

Jackendoff, R. (2002). *Foundations of language*. Oxford: Oxford University Press.

Jones, E. A., Carr, E. G., & Feeley, K. M. (2006). Multiple effects of joint attention intervention for children with autism. *Behavior Modification, 30*, 782–834.

Kaiser, A. P., & Roberts, M. Y. (2011). Advances in early communication and language intervention. *Journal of Early Intervention, 33*, 298–309.

Karmiloff, K., & Karmiloff-Smith, A. (2001). *Pathways to language: From fetus to adolescent*. Cambridge, MA: Harvard University Press.

Karmiloff-Smith, A. (2005). Bates's emergentist theory and its relevance to understanding genotype/phenotype relations. In M. Tomasello & D. I. Slobin (Eds), *Beyond nature-nurture: Essays in honor of Elizabeth Bates*. (pp. 219–236). Mahwah, NJ: Erlbaum.

Karmiloff-Smith, A. (2011). Static snapshots versus dynamic approaches to genes, brain, cognition and behaviour in neurodevelopmental disabilities. *International Review of Research in Developmental Disabilities, 40*, 1–16.

Kay-Raining Bird, E., Cleave, P., Trudeau, N., Thordardottir, E., Sutton, A., & Thorpe, A. (2005). The language abilities of bilingual children with Down syndrome. *American Journal of Speech–Language Pathology, 14*, 187–199.

Kay-Raining Bird, E., Genese, F., & Verhoeven, L. (2016). Bilingualism in children with developmental disorders: A narrative review. *Journal of Communication Disorders, 63*, 1–14.

Kaye, K., & Fogel, A. (1980). The temporal structure of face-to-face communication between mothers and infants. *Developmental Psychology, 16*, 454–464.

Kegl, J., & Iwata, G. (1989). Lenguaje de Signos Nicaragüense: A pidgin sheds light on the "creole?" ASL. In R. Carlson, S. DeLancey, S. Gilden, D. Payne & A. Saxena (Eds), *Proceedings of the Fourth Annual Meeting of the Pacific Linguistics Conference* (pp. 266–294). Eugene, OR: University of Oregon.

Keil, F. C. (1986). Conceptual domains and the acquisition of metaphor. *Cognitive Development, 1*, 72–96.

Kendon, A. (2004). *Gesture: Visible action as utterance*. Cambridge: Cambridge University Press.

Kerbel, D., & Grunwell, P. (1998a). A study of idiom comprehension in children with semantic-pragmatic difficulties. Part I: Task effects on the assessment of idiom comprehension in children. *International Journal of Language and Communication Disorders, 33*, 1–22.

Kerbel, D., & Grunwell, P. (1998b). A study of idiom comprehension in children with semantic-pragmatic difficulties. Part II: Between-groups results and discussion. *International Journal of Language and Communication Disorders, 33*, 23–44.

Kim, S. H., & Lord, C. (2013). The behavioral manifestations of autism spectrum disorders. In J. D. Buxbaum & P. R. Hof (Eds), The *neuroscience of autism spectrum disorders* (pp. 25–37). Amsterdam, NL: Elsevier.

Kimura, D. (1999). *Sex and cognition*. Cambridge, MA: MIT Press.

Kohnert, K. (2010). Bilingual children with primary language impairment: Issues, evidence and implications for clinical actions. *Journal of Communication Disorders, 43*, 456–473.

Kuczaj II, S. A. (1982). Language play and language acquisition. *Advances in Child Development and Behavior, 17*, 197–232.

Kuehn, D. P., & Moller, K. T. (2000). The state of the art: Speech and language issues in the cleft palate population. *The Cleft Palate-Craniofacial Journal, 37*, 1–35.

Kuhl, P. K. (1992). Psychoacoustics and speech perception: Internal standards, perceptual anchors, and prototypes. In L. A. Werner & E. W. Rubel (Eds), *Developmental Psychoacoustics* (pp. 293–332). Washington, DC: American Psychological Association.

Kuhl, P. K. (1993). Early linguistic experience and phonetic perception: Implications for theories of developmental speech perception. *Journal of Phonetics, 21*, 125–139.

Kuhl, P. K. (2010). Brain mechanisms in early language acquisition. *Neuron, 67*, 713–727.

Küntay, A. C. (2004). Lists as alternative discourse structures to narratives in preschool children's conversations. *Discourse Processes, 38*, 95–118.

Labov, W. (1972). The transformation of reality in narrative syntax. In W. Labov (Ed.), *Language in the inner city* (pp. 354–396). Philadelphia, PA: University of Pennsylvania Press.

Labov, W., & Labov, T. (1978). *The phonetics of cat and mama*. Language, *54*, 816–852.

Ladefoged, P. (2004). *Vowels and consonants*. Oxford: Blackwell.

Ladegaard, H. J., & Bleses, D. (2003). Gender differences in young children's speech: The acquisition of sociolinguistic competence. *International Journal of Applied Linguistics, 13*, 222–233.

Lakoff, G. (1987). *Women, fire and dangerous things.* Chicago, IL: University of Chicago Press.

Lanza, E. (1997). *Language mixing in infant bilingualism: A sociolinguistic perspective.* Oxford: Clarendon Press.

Launonen, K. (1996). Enhancing communication skills of children with Down syndrome: Early use of manual signs. In S. von Tetzchner & M. H. Jensen (Eds), *Augmentative and alternative communication: European perspectives* (pp. 213–231). London: Whurr/Wiley.

Law, J., Gaag, A., Hardcastle, W. J., Beckett, D. J., MacGregor, A., & Plunkett, C. (2007). *Communication support needs: A review of the literature.* Edinburgh: Scottish Executive.

Leaper, C., & Smith, T. E. (2004). A meta-analytic review of gender variations in children's language use: Talkativeness, affiliative speech, and assertive speech. *Developmental Psychology, 40,* 993–1027.

Lederer, S. H., & Battaglia, D. (2015). Using signs to facilitate vocabulary in children with language delays. *Infants and Young Children, 28,* 18–31.

Legerstee, M., & Barillas, Y. (2003). Sharing attention and pointing to objects at 12 months: Is the intentional stance implied? *Cognitive Development, 18,* 91–110.

Levorato, M. C., & Cacciari, C. (2002). The creation of new figurative expressions: Psycholinguistic evidence on children, adolescents and adults. *Journal of Child Language, 29,* 127–150.

Lewis, M. M. (1936). *Infant speech.* London: Routledge and Kegan Paul.

Li, P., Huang, B., & Hsiao, Y. (2010). Learning that classifiers count: Mandarin-speaking children's acquisition of sortal and mensural classifiers. *Journal of East Asian Linguistics, 19,* 207–230.

Lieven, E. (2014). First language development: A usage-based perspective on past and current research. *Journal of Child Language, 41,* 48–63.

Lieven, E. (2016). Usage-based approaches to language development: Where do we go from here? *Language and Cognition, 8,* 346–368.

Lieven, E., Behrens, H., Speares, J., & Tomasello, M. (2003). Early syntactic creativity: A usage-based approach. *Journal of Child Language, 30,* 333–370.

Lieven, E., Salomo, D., & Tomasello, M. (2009). Two-year-old children's production of multiword utterances: A usage-based analysis. *Cognitive Linguistics, 20,* 481–508.

Lisina, M. I. (1985). *Child, adults, peers: Patterns of communication.* Moscow: Progress Publishers.

Liszkowski, U., Carpenter, M., Striano, T., & Tomasello, M. (2006). Twelve- and 18-month-olds point to provide information for others. *Journal of Cognition and Development, 7,* 173–187.

Lloyd, P., Camaioni, L., & Ercolani, P. (1995). Assessing referential communication skills in the primary school years: A comparative study. *British Journal of Developmental Psychology, 13,* 13–29.

Lock, A. (1980). *The guided reinvention of language*. London: Academic Press.

Lock, A., Young, A., Service, V., & Chandler, P. (1990). Some observations on the origin of the pointing gesture. In V. Volterra & C. Erting (Eds), *From gesture to language in hearing and deaf children* (pp. 42–55). Berlin: Springer.

Lu, J., Jones, A., & Morgan, G. (2016). The impact of input quality on early sign development in native and non-native language learners. *Journal of Child Language*, *43*, 537–552.

Lund, E. M., Kohlmeier, T. L., & Durán, L. K. (2017). Comparative language development in bilingual and monolingual children with autism spectrum disorder: A systematic review. *Journal of Early Intervention*, *39*, 106–124.

Lundervold, A. J., Heimann, M., & Manger, T. (2008). Behaviour–emotional characteristics of primary-school children rated as having language problems. *British Journal of Educational Psychology*, *78*, 567–580.

MacPherson, A. C., & Moore, C. (2007). Attentional control by gaze cues in infancy. In R. Flom, K. Lee & D. Muir (Eds), *Gaze-following: Its development and significance* (pp. 53–75). Mahwah, NJ: Lawrence Erlbaum.

MacWhinney, B. (1982). Basic syntactic processes. In S. Kuczaj (Ed.), *Language development. Volume 1. Syntax and semantics* (pp. 73–136). Hillsdale, NJ: Erlbaum.

MacWhinney, B. (2015). Language development. In R. M. Lerner, L. Liben & U. Muller (Eds), *Handbook of child psychology and developmental science, Seventh edition, Volume 2: Cognitive processes* (pp. 296–338). New York, NY: Wiley.

MacWhinney, B., & O'Grady, W. (Eds) (2015). *Handbook of language emergence*. New York, NY: Wiley.

Majid, A., Boster, J. S., & Bowerman, M. (2008). The cross-linguistic categorization of everyday events: A study of cutting and breaking. *Cognition*, *109*, 235–250.

Marcus, G. F. (1995). Children's overregularization of English plurals: A quantitative analysis. *Journal of Child Language*, *22*, 447–459.

Marinova-Todd, S. H., Colozzo, P., Mirenda, P., Stahl, H., Kay-Raining Bird, E., Parkington, K., Cain, K., Scherba de Valenzuela, J., Segers, E., MacLeod, A. A., & Genesee, F. (2016). Professional practices and opinions about services available to bilingual children with developmental disabilities: An international study. *Journal of Communication Disorders*, *63*, 47–62.

Markman, E. M. (1992). Constraints on word learning: Speculations about their nature, origins and domain specificity. In M. R. Gunnar & M. P. Maratsos (Eds), *Minnesota symposia on child psychology*, Volume *25* (pp. 59–101). Hillsdale, NJ: Lawrence Erlbaum.

Masataka, N. (1992). Motherese in a signed language. *Infant Behavior and Development*, *15*, 453–460.

Masur, E. F. (1997). Maternal labelling of novel and familiar objects: Implications for children's development of lexical constraints. *Journal of Child Language*, *24*, 427–439.

Maurer, D., & Werker, J. F. (2014). Perceptual narrowing during infancy: A comparison of language and faces. *Developmental Psychobiology, 56,* 154–178.

McAndrew, B., & Malley-Keighran, M. P. O. (2017). "She didn't have a word of English; we didn't have a word of Vietnamese": Exploring parent experiences of communication with toddlers who were adopted internationally. *Journal of Communication Disorders, 68,* 89–102.

McGillion, M., Herbert, J. S., Pine, J., Vihman, M., DePaolis, R., Keren-Portnoy, T., & Matthews, D. (2017). What paves the way to conventional language? The predictive value of babble, pointing, and socioeconomic status. *Child Development, 88,* 156–166.

McLeod, S., & Bleile, K. (2003, November). *Neurological and developmental foundations of speech acquisition.* Invited seminar presentation at the annual convention of the American Speech-Language-Hearing Association, Chicago, IL.

McQueen, J. M., Tyler, M. D., & Cutler, A. (2012). Lexical retuning of children's speech perception: Evidence for knowledge about words' component sounds. *Language Learning and Development, 8,* 317–339.

Mellon, N. K., Niparko, J. K., Rathmann, C., Mathur, G., Humphries, T., Napoli, D. J., Handley, T., Scambler, S., & Lantos, J. D. (2015). Should all deaf children learn sign language? *Pediatrics, 136,* 170–176.

Merriman, W. E. (1986). Some reasons for the occurrence and eventual correction of children's naming errors. *Child Development, 57,* 942–952.

Millar, D. C., Light, J. C., & Schlosser, R. W. (2006). The impact of augmentative and alternative communication intervention on the speech production of individuals with developmental disabilities: A research review. *Journal of Speech, Language, and Hearing Research, 49,* 248–264.

Miller, P. (2010). Phonological, orthographic, and syntactic awareness and their relation to reading comprehension in prelingually deaf individuals: what can we learn from skilled readers? Journal of Development and Physical Disabilities, 22, 549–580.

Miller, J. F. (Ed.) (1981). *Assessing children's language production: Experimental procedures.* Baltimore: University Park Press.

Mirenda, P. (1997). Supporting individuals with challenging behavior through functional communication training and AAC: Research review. *Augmentative and Alternative Communication, 13,* 207–225.

Moe, S., & Wright, M. (2013, July). Can accessible digital formats improve reading skills, habits and educational level for dyslectic youngsters? In C. Stephanidis & M. Antona (Eds), Universal access in human-computer interaction. Applications and services for quality of life. UAHCI 2013. *Lecture Notes in Computer Science,* vol *8011* (pp. 203–212). Heidelberg, Germany: Springer.

Morris, D., Collett, P., Marsh, P., & O'Shaughnessy, M. (1979). *Gestures: Their origin and distribution.* London: Cape.

Mundy, P., Block, J., Delgado, C., Pomares, Y., Van Hecke, A. V., & Parlade, M. V. (2007). Individual differences and the development of joint attention in infancy. *Child Development, 78,* 938–954.

Muris, P., & Ollendick, T. H. (2015). Children who are anxious in silence: A review on selective mutism, the new anxiety disorder in DSM-5. *Clinical Child and Family Psychology Review, 18*, 151–169.

Murza, K. A., Schwartz, J. B., Hahs-Vaughn, D. L., & Nye, C. (2016). Joint attention interventions for children with autism spectrum disorder: A systematic review and meta-analysis. *International Journal of Language and Communication Disorders, 51*, 236–251.

Naber, F. B. A., Bakermans-Kranenburg, M. J., van IJzendoorn, M. H., Dietz, C., van Daalen, E., Swinkels, S. H. N., Buitelaar, J. K., & van Engeland, H. (2008). Joint attention development in toddlers with autism. *European Child and Adolescent Psychiatry, 17*, 143–152.

Nagy, W. E., & Anderson, R. C. (1984). How many words are there in printed school English? *Reading Research Quarterly, 19*, 304–330.

Nagy, W. E., & Townsend, D. (2012). Words as tools: Learning academic vocabulary as language acquisition. *Reading Research Quarterly, 47*, 91–108.

Namy, L. L., & Waxman, S. R. (1998). Words and gestures: Infants' interpretations of different forms of symbolic reference. *Child Development, 69*, 295–308.

Napier, J., Leigh, G., & Nann, S. (2007). Teaching sign language to hearing parents of deaf children: An action research process. *Deafness and Education International, 9*, 83–100.

Nelson, K. (1973). Structure and strategy in learning to talk. *Monographs of the Society for Research in Child Development, 38*.

Nelson, K. (1981). Individual differences in language development: Implications for development and language. *Developmental Psychology, 17*, 170–187.

Nelson, K. (1988). Constraints on word learning? *Cognitive Development, 3*, 221–246.

Nelson, K. (2007a). *Young minds in social worlds: Experience, meaning and memory.* Cambridge, MA: Harvard University Press.

Nelson, K. (2007b). Development of extended memory. *Journal of Physiology, 101*, 223–229.

Nelson, K. (2009). Wittgenstein and contemporary theories of word learning. *New Ideas in Psychology, 27*, 275–287.

Nelson, K., & Gruendel, J. M. (1979). At morning it's lunchtime: A scriptal view of children's dialogues. *Discourse Processes, 3*, 73–94.

Nelson, K. E. (2001). Dynamic tricky mix theory suggests multiple analyzed pathways as an intervention approach for children with autism and other language delays. In S. von Tetzchner & J. Clibbens (Eds), *Understanding the theoretical and methodological bases of augmentative and alternative communication. Proceedings of the Sixth Biennial Research Symposium of the International Society of Augmentative and Alternative Communication (ISAAC), Washington, DC, August 2000* (pp. 141–159). Toronto, Canada: ISAAC.

Nelson, K. E., Carskaddon, G., & Bonvillian, J. D. (1973). Syntax acquisition: Impact of experimental variation in adult verbal interaction with the child. *Child Development, 44*, 497–504.

Nicolopoulou, A., & Richner, E. S. (2007). From actors to agents to persons: The development of character representation in young children's narratives. *Child Development, 78*, 412–429.

Nippold, M. A. (1998). *Later language development, Second edition.* Austin, TX: Pro-Ed.

Nippold, M. A., Frantz-Kaspar, M. W., Cramond, P. M., Kirk, C., Hayward-Mayhew, C., & MacKinnon, M. (2014). Conversational and narrative speaking in adolescents: Examining the use of complex syntax. *Journal of Speech, Language, and Hearing Research, 57*, 876–886.

Norbury, C. F., & Bishop, D. V. (2003). Narrative skills of children with communication impairments. *International Journal of Language and Communication Disorders, 38*, 287–313.

Novak, G., & Peláez, M. (2004). *Child and adolescent development: A behavioral systems approach.* London: Sage.

Novogrodsky, R., Henner, J., Caldwell-Harris, C., & Hoffmeister, R. (2017). The development of sensitivity to grammatical violations in American Sign Language: Native versus nonnative signers. *Language Learning, 67*, 791–818.

O'Neill, Y. V. (1980). *Speech and speech disorders in Western thought before 1600.* London: Greenwood Press.

Ostad, J. (2008). *Zweisprachigkeit bei Kindern mit Down-Syndrom.* Hamburg: Verlag Dr. Kovač.

Özçalișkan. S., & Goldin-Meadow, S. (2010). Sex differences in language first appear in gesture. *Developmental Science, 13*, 752–760.

Pan, B. A., & Snow, C. E. (1999). The development of conversational and discourse skills. In M. Barrett. (Ed.), *Development of Language* (pp. 229–249). Hove, UK: Psychology Press.

Paradis, J. (2010). The interface between bilingual development and specific language impairment. *Applied Psycholinguistics, 31*, 227–252.

Parish-Morris, J., Mahajan, N., Hirsh-Pasek, K., Golinkoff, R. M., & Collins, M. F. (2013). Once upon a time: Parent–child dialogue and storybook reading in the electronic era. *Mind, Brain, and Education, 7*, 200–211.

Paul, R., Hernandez, R., Taylor, L., & Johnson, K. (1996). Narrative development in late talkers: Early school age. *Journal of Speech, Language, and Hearing Research, 39*, 1295–1303.

Peña, E. D. (2016). Supporting the home language of bilingual children with developmental disabilities: From knowing to doing. *Journal of Communication Disorders, 63*, 85–92.

Pérez-Pereira, M., & Conti-Ramsden, G. (1999). *Language development and social interaction in blind children.* Hove, UK: Psychology Press.

Peters, A. M. (1995). Strategies in the acquisition of syntax. In P. Fletcher & B. MacWhinney (Eds), *The handbook of child language* (pp. 462–482). Oxford: Basil Blackwell.

Petersen, D. B. (2011). A systematic review of narrative-based language intervention with children who have language impairment. *Communication Disorders Quarterly, 32*, 207–220.

Petersen, D. B., Brown, C. L., Ukrainetz, T. A., Wise, C., Spencer, T. D., & Zebre, J. (2014). Systematic individualized narrative language intervention on the personal narratives of children with autism. *Language, Speech, and Hearing Services in Schools, 45*, 67–86.

Petersen, D. B., & Spencer, T. D. (2016). Using narrative intervention to accelerate canonical story grammar and complex language growth in culturally diverse preschoolers. *Topics in Language Disorders, 36*, 6–19.

Petitto, L. A. (1992). Modularity and constraints in early lexical acquisition: Evidence from children's early language and gesture. In M. R. Gunnar & M. Maratsos (Eds), *Minnesota symposium on child psychology*, Volume *25* (pp. 25–58). Hillsdale, NJ: Lawrence Erlbaum.

Petitto, L. A., Katerelos, M., Levy, B. G., Gauna, K., Tetreault, K., & Ferraro, V. (2001). Bilingual signed and spoken language acquisition from birth: Implications for the mechanisms underlying early bilingual language acquisition. *Journal of Child Language, 28*, 453–496.

Petitto, L. A., & Marentette, P. F. (1991). Babbling in the manual mode: Evidence for the ontogeny of language. *Science, 251*, 1493–1496.

Petretic, P. A., & Tweney, R. D. (1977). Does comprehension precede the production? The development of children's responses to telegraphic sentences of varying grammatical adequacy. *Journal of Child Language, 4*, 201–209.

Pinker, S. (1994). *The language instinct*. London: Allen Lane.

Pizer, G., Walters, K., & Meier R. P. (2007). Bringing up baby with baby signs: Language ideologies and socialization in hearing families. *Sign Language Studies, 7*, 387–430.

Poulin-Dubois, D., & Graham, S. A. (1994). Infant categorization and early object–word meaning. In A. Vyt, H. Bloch & M. H. Bornstein (Eds), *Early child development in the French tradition: Contributions from current research* (pp. 207–225). Hillsdale, NJ: Erlbaum.

Pramling, N. (2015). Learning and metaphor: Bridging the gap between the familiar and the unfamiliar. In M. Fleer & N. Pramling (Eds), *A cultural-historical study of children learning science* (pp. 125–132). Dordrecht, The Netherlands: Springer.

Radford, A. (1990). *Syntactic theory and the acquisition of English syntax*. Cambridge, MA: Blackwell.

Rakova, M. (2003). *The extent of the literal: Metaphor, polysemy and theories of concepts*. Basingstoke, UK: Palgrave Macmillan.

Ramer, A. (1976). Syntactic styles in emerging language. *Journal of Child Language, 3*, 49–62.

Reznick, J. S., & Goldfield, B. A. (1992). Rapid change in lexical development in comprehension and production. *Developmental Psychology, 28*, 406–413.

Rinaldi, P., Caselli, M. C., Di Renzo, A., Gulli, T., & Volterra, V. (2014). Sign vocabulary in deaf toddlers exposed to sign language since birth. *Journal of Deaf Studies and Deaf Education, 19*, 303–318.

Rommetveit, R. (1974). *On message structure.* London: Wiley.

Rowe, M. L. (2012). A longitudinal investigation of the role of quantity and quality of child-directed speech in vocabulary development. *Child Development, 83*, 1762–1774.

Sachs, J., & Truswell, L. (1978). Comprehension of two word instructions by children in the one word stage. *Journal of Child Language, 5*, 17–24.

Sarria, E., Gomez, J. C., & Tamarit, J. (1996). Joint attention and alternative language intervention in autism: Implications of theory for practice. In S. von Tetzchner & M. H. Jensen (Eds), *Augmentative and alternative communication: European perspectives* (pp. 49–64). London: Whurr/Wiley.

Saunders, G. (1988). *Bilingual children: From birth to teens.* Clevedon, OH: Multilingual Matters.

Schaadt, G., Hesse, V., & Friederici, A. D. (2015). Sex hormones in early infancy seem to predict aspects of later language development. *Brain and Language, 141*, 70–76.

Schaffer, H. R. (1989). Language development in context. In S. von Tetzchner, L. S. Siegel & L. Smith (Eds), *The social and cognitive aspects of normal and atypical language development* (pp. 1–22). New York, NY: Springer.

Scheidnes, M., & Tuller, L. (2016). Assessing successive bilinguals in two languages: A longitudinal look at English-speaking children in France. *Journal of Communication Disorders, 64*, 45–61.

Schiavo, G., & Buson, V. (2014). Interactive e-books to support reading skills in dyslexia. Presented at IBOOC 2014—2nd Workshop on Interactive eBook for Children at IDC 2014.

Schley, S., & Snow, C. E. (1992). The conversational skills of school aged children. *Social Development, 1*, 18–35.

Schlosser, R. W., & Wendt, O. (2008). Effects of augmentative and alternative communication intervention on speech production in children with autism: A systematic review. *American Journal of Speech-Language Pathology, 17*, 212–230.

Schober-Peterson, D., & Johnson, C. J. (1991). Non-dialogue speech during preschool interactions. *Journal of Child Language, 18*, 153–170.

Scollon, R. T. (1976). *Conversations with a one year old.* Honolulu: University of Hawaii Press.

Scollon, R. T. (2001). *Mediated discourse: The nexus of practice.* London: Routledge.

Scott, S., & Beidel, D. C. (2011). Selective mutism: An update and suggestions for future research. *Current Psychiatry Reports, 13*, 251–257.

Shatz, M., & Gelman, R. (1973). The development of communication skills: Modification in the speech of young children as a function of the listener. *Monographs of the Society for Research in Child Development, 38*.

Shatz, M., & O'Reilly, A. W. (1990). Conversational or communicative skill? A reassessment of two year olds' behaviour in miscommunication episodes. *Journal of Child Language*, *17*, 131–146.

Shinn, M. W. (1900). *The biography of a baby*. New York, NY: Miffli.

Silva, M., Straesser, K., & Cain, K. (2014). Early narrative skills in Chilean preschool: Questions scaffold the production of coherent narratives. *Early Childhood Research Quarterly*, *29*, 205–213.

Skinner, B. F. (1957). *Verbal behavior*. New York, NY: Appleton-Century-Crofts.

Slobin, D. I. (1973). Cognitive prerequisites for development of grammar. In C. A. Ferguson & D. I. Slobin (Eds), *Studies of child language development* (pp. 175–208). New York, NY: Holt, Rinehart and Winston.

Smith, M. M., & Murray, J. (Eds) (2016). *The silent partner? Language, interaction and aided communication*. Albury, UK: J&R Press.

Snow, C. E. (1977). Mothers' speech research: From input to interaction. In C. E. Snow & C. A. Ferguson (Eds), *Talking to children* (pp. 31–49). Cambridge: Cambridge University Press.

Snow, C. E. (2010). Academic language and the challenge of reading for learning about science. *Science*, *328* (*5977*), 450–452.

Snow, C. E., Pan, B., Imbens-Bailey, A., & Herman, J. (1996). Learning how to say what one means: A longitudinal study of children's speech act use. *Social Development*, *5*, 56–84.

Soto, G., & Hartmann, E. (2006). Analysis of narratives produced by four children who use augmentative and alternative communication. *Journal of Communication Disorders*, *39*, 456–480.

Southgate, V., Van Maanen, C., & Csibra, G. (2007). Infant pointing: Communication to cooperate or communication to learn? *Child Development*, *78*, 735–740.

Spencer, P. E., & Harris, M. (2006). Patterns and effects of language input to deaf infants and toddlers from Deaf and hearing mothers. In B. Schick, M. Marschark & P. E. Spencer (Eds), *Advances in sign language development of deaf children* (pp. 71–101). New York, NY: Oxford University Press.

Spinelli, M., Fasolo, M., & Mesman, J. (2017). Does prosody make the difference? A meta-analysis on relations between prosodic aspects of infant-directed speech and infant outcomes. *Developmental Review*, *44*, 1–18.

Stadskleiv, K., Jahnsen, R., Andersen, G. L., & von Tetzchner, S. (2017). Neuropsychological profiles of children with cerebral palsy. *Developmental Neurorehabilitation*, *28*, 108–120.

Stenberg, N., Bresnahan, M., Gunnes, N., Hirtz, D., Hornig, M., Lie, K. K., Lipkin, W. I., Lord, C., Magnus, P., Reichborn-Kjennerud, T., et al. (2014). Identifying children with autism spectrum disorder at 18 months in a general population sample. *Paediatric and Perinatal Epidemiology*, *28*, 255–262.

Strange, W., & Broen, P. A. (1980). Perception and production of approximant consonants by 3-year-olds: A first study. In G. H. Yeni-Komshian, J. F. Kavanagh & C. A. Ferguson (Eds), *Child phonology. Volume 2: Perception* (pp. 117–154). New York, NY: Academic Press.

Strohner, H., & Nelson, K. E. (1974). The young child's development of sentence comprehension: Influence of event probability, nonverbal context, syntactic form, and strategies. *Child Development, 45*, 567–576.

Strong, M., & Prinz, P. M. (1997). A study of the relationship between American Sign Language and English literacy. *The Journal of Deaf Studies and Deaf Education, 2*, 37–46.

Tardif, T. (1996). Nouns are not always learned before verbs: Evidence from Mandarin speakers' early vocabularies. *Developmental Psychology, 32*, 492–504.

Tardif, T. (2006). But are they really verbs? Chinese words for action. In K. Hirsh-Pasek & R. M. Golinkoff (Eds), *Action meets word: How children learn verbs* (pp. 477–498). New York, NY: Oxford University Press.

Tardif, T., Fletcher, P., Liang, W., Zhang, Z., Kaciroti, N., & Marchman, V. A. (2008). Baby's first 10 words. *Developmental Psychology, 44*, 929–938.

Tenenbaum, H. R., Ford, S., & Alkhedairy, B. (2011). Telling stories: Gender differences in peers' emotion talk and communication style. *British Journal of Developmental Psychology, 29*, 707–721.

Terrace, H. S. (1979). *Nim: A chimpanzee who learned sign language.* New York, NY: Washington Square Press.

Thorne, S. L., & Tasker, T. (2011). Sociocultural and cultural-historical theories of language development. In J. Simpson (Ed.), *Routledge handbook of applied linguistics* (pp. 487–500). New York, NY: Routledge.

Thorseng, L. A. (1997). *Danske & engelske børns tilegnelse av termer for rumlige relasjoner: En kognitiv lingvistisk undersøgelse.* Doctoral dissertation, Aarhus University.

Tomasello, M. (1992). *First verbs.* Cambridge: Cambridge University Press.

Tomasello, M. (1995). Language is not an instinct. *Cognitive Development, 10*, 131–156.

Tomasello, M. (1999). *The cultural origins of human cognition.* London: Harvard University Press.

Tomasello, M. (2003). *Constructing a language. A usage-based theory of language acquisition.* London: Harvard University Press.

Tomasello, M. (2005). "Cultural constraints on grammar and cognition in Piraha: Another look at the design features of human language": Comment. *Current Anthropology, 46*, 640–641.

Tomasello, M. (2006). Acquiring linguistic constructions. In W. Damon, R. M. Lerner, D. Kuhn & R. S. Siegler (Eds), *Handbook of child psychology, Sixth edition, Volume 2: Cognition, perception and language* (pp. 371–384). New York, NY: Wiley.

Tomasello, M. (2008). *The origins of human communication.* Cambridge, MA: MIT Press.

Tomasello, M. (2009). *Why we cooperate.* London: MIT Press.

Tomasello, M., & Akhtar, N. (1995). Two-year-olds use pragmatic cues to differentiate reference to objects and actions. *Cognitive Development, 10*, 201–224.

Tomasello, M., & Camaioni, L. (1997). A comparison of the gestural communication of apes and human infants. *Human Development, 40*, 7–24.

Tomasello, M., Carpenter, M., & Lizskowski, U. (2007). A new look at infant pointing. *Child Development, 78,* 705–722.

Trevarthen, C. (1979). Communication and cooperation in early infancy: A description of primary intersubjectivity. In M. Bullowa (Ed.), *Before speech* (pp. 321–347). Cambridge: Cambridge University Press.

Trevarthen, C. (2015). Infant semiosis: The psycho-biology of action and shared experience from birth. *Cognitive Development, 36,* 130–141.

Ukrainetz, T. A., Justice, L. M., Kadaravek, J. N., Eisenberg, S. N., Gillam, R. B., & Horn, M. (2005). The development of expressive elaboration in fictional narratives. *Journal of Speech, Language, and Hearing Research, 48,* 1363–1377.

van Bysterveldt, A. K., Westerveld, M. F., Gillon, G., & Foster-Cohen, S. (2012). Personal narrative skills of school-aged children with Down syndrome. *International Journal of Language and Communication Disorders, 47,* 95–105.

van Daal, J., Verhoeven, L., & van Balkom, H. (2007). Behaviour problems in children with language impairment. *Journal of Child Psychology and Psychiatry, 48,* 1139–1147.

Veneziano, E. (2016). The development of narrative discourse in French by 5 to 10 years old children: Some insights from a conversational interaction method. In J. Perera, M. Aparici, E. Rosado & N. Salas (Eds), *Written and spoken language development across the lifespan: Essays in honour of Liliana Tolchinsky* (pp. 141–160). New York, NY: Springer.

Verdon, S., Wong, S., & McLeod, S. (2016). Shared knowledge and mutual respect: Enhancing culturally competent practice through collaboration with families and communities. *Child Language Teaching and Therapy, 32,* 205–221.

Vihman, M. (1993). Variable paths to early word production. *Journal of Phonetics, 21,* 61–82.

Vogt, P., & Lieven, E. (2010). Verifying theories of language acquisition using computer models of language evolution. *Adaptive Behavior, 18,* 21–35.

von Tetzchner, S. (2018). Introduction to the special issue on aided language processes, development, and use: An international perspective. *Augmentative and Alternative Communication, 34,* 1–15.

von Tetzchner, S., & Grove, N. (Eds) (2003). *Augmentative and alternative communication: Developmental issues.* London: Whurr/Wiley.

von Tetzchner, S., Hoiting, N., Küntay, A. C., & Slobin, D. I. (2008). Variation sets in child-directed language – implication for intervention with alternative means of communication. Presented at 13th Biennial Conference of the International Society for Augmentative and Alternative Communication, Montreal, Canada, 4–9 August, 2008.

von Tetzchner, S., & Martinsen, H. (2000). *Introduction to augmentative and alternative communication.* London: Whurr/Wiley.

von Tetzchner, S., & Sedberg, T. (2005). Young blind children in activities with joint attention. Presented at X. International Conference for the Study of Child Language, Berlin, Germany, 25–29 July 2005.

von Tetzchner, S., & Stadskleiv, K. (2016). Constructing a language in alternative forms, In M. M. Smith & J. Murray (Eds), *The silent partner? Language, interaction and aided communication* (pp. 17–34). Guildford, UK: J&R Press

Vygotsky, L. S. (1962). *Thought and language.* Cambridge, MA: MIT Press.

Wagner, K. R. (1985). How much do children say in a day? *Journal of Child Language, 12,* 475–487.

Waxman, S. R., & Braun, I. (2005). Consistent (but not variable) names as invitations to form categories: New evidence from 12-month-old infants. *Cognition, 95,* B59–B68

Weisleder, A., & Fernald, A. (2013). Talking to children matters: Early language experience strengthens processing and builds vocabulary. *Psychological Science, 24,* 2143–2152.

Werker, J. F. (1991). The ontogeny of speech perception. In G. Mattingly & M. Studdert-Kennedy (Eds), *Modularity and the motor theory of speech perception* (pp. 91–109). Hillsdale, NJ: Erlbaum.

Werker, J. F., & Byers-Heinlein, K. (2008). Bilingualism in infancy: First steps in perception and comprehension. *Trends in Cognitive Sciences, 12,* 144–151.

Westermann, G., Ruh, G., & Plunkett, K. (2009). Connectionist approaches to language learning. *Linguistics, 47,* 413–452.

Wexler, K. (1999). Maturation and growth of grammar. In W. C. Ritchie & T. K. Bhatia (Eds), *Handbook of child language acquisition* (pp. 55–109). London: Academic Press.

Winner, E. (1988). *The point of words: Children's understanding of metaphor and irony.* Cambridge, MA: Harvard University Press.

Woodward, A. L., & Markman, L. (1998). Early word learning. In W. Damon, D. Kuhn & R. S. Siegler (Eds), *Handbook of child psychology, Fifth edition, Volume 2: Cognition, perception and language* (pp. 371–420). New York, NY: Wiley.

Wright, C. A., Kaiser, A. P., Reikowsky, D. I., & Roberts, M. Y. (2013). Effects of a naturalistic sign intervention on expressive language of toddlers with Down syndrome. *Journal of Speech, Language, and Hearing Research, 56,* 994–1008.

Wunderlich, D. (2004). Why assume UG? *Studies in Language. International Journal sponsored by the Foundation "Foundations of Language", 28,* 615–641.

Xu, F. (2002). The role of language in acquiring object kind concepts in infancy. *Cognition, 85,* 223–250.

Yu, B. (2013). Issues in bilingualism and heritage language maintenance: Perspectives of minority-language mothers of children with autism spectrum disorders. *American Journal of Speech-Language Pathology, 22,* 10–24.

Yu, B. (2016a). Bilingualism as conceptualized and bilingualism as lived: A critical examination of the monolingual socialization of a child with autism in a bilingual family. *Journal of Autism and Developmental Disorders, 46,* 424–435.

Yu, B. (2016b). Code-switching as a communicative resource within routine, bilingual family interactions for a child on the autism spectrum. *Perspectives of the ASHA Special Interest Groups, 1,* 17–28.

Zambrana, I. M., Ystrom, E., & Pons, F. (2012). Impact of gender, maternal education, and birth order on the development of language comprehension: A longitudinal study from 18 to 36 months of age. *Journal of Developmental and Behavioral Pediatrics, 33*, 146–155.

Zevenbergen, A. A., Holmes, A., Haman, E., Whiteford, N., & Thielges, S. (2016). Variability in mothers' support for preschoolers' contributions to co-constructed narratives as a function of child age. *First Language, 36*, 601–616.

Index

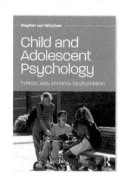

The **Topics from Child and Adolescent Psychology Series** is drawn from Stephen von Tetzchner's comprehensive textbook for all students of developmental psychology *Child and Adolescent Psychology: Typical and Atypical Development*

Table of Contents

Praise for *Child and Adolescent Psychology: Typical and Atypical Development*

'An extensive overview of the field of developmental psychology. It illustrates how knowledge about typical and atypical development can be integrated and used to highlight fundamental processes of human growth and maturation.'

Dr. John Coleman, *PhD, OBE, UK*

'A broad panoply of understandings of development from a wide diversity of perspectives and disciplines, spanning all the key areas, and forming a comprehensive, detailed and extremely useful text for students and practitioners alike'.

Dr. Graham Music, *Consultant Psychotherapist,*
Tavistock Clinic London, UK

'An extraordinary blend of depth of scholarship with a lucid, and engaging, writing style. Its coverage is impressive . . . Both new and advanced students will love the coverage of this text.'

Professor Joseph Campos, *University of California, USA*

'Encyclopedic breadth combined with an unerring eye for the central research across developmental psychology, particularly for the period of its explosive growth since the 1960s. Both a text and a reference work, this will be the go-to resource for any teacher, researcher or student of the discipline for the foreseeable future.'

Professor Andy Lock, *University of Lisbon, Portugal*

It is accompanied by a companion website featuring chapter summaries, glossary, quizzes and instructor resources.

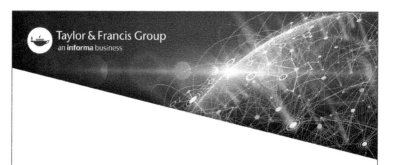

www.ingramcontent.com/pod-product-compliance
Ingram Content Group UK Ltd.
Pitfield, Milton Keynes, MK11 3LW, UK
UKHW020347010325
455677UK00020B/327